REASONS TO BE PRETTY

"Mr. LaBute is writing some of the freshest and most illuminating American dialogue to be heard anywhere these days . . . *reasons* flows with the compelling naturalness of overheard conversation. . . . It's never easy to say what you mean, or to know what you mean to begin with. With a delicacy that belies its crude vocabulary, *reasons to be pretty* celebrates the everyday heroism in the struggle to find out." —**Ben Brantley**, *The New York Times*

"[T]here is no doubt that LaBute knows how to hold an audience. . . . LaBute proves just as interesting writing about human decency as when he is writing about the darker urgings of the human heart." —**Charles Spencer**, *Telegraph*

"[F]unny, daring, thought-provoking . . ." —**Sarah Hemming**, *Financial Times*

IN A DARK DARK HOUSE

"Refreshingly reminds us . . . that [LaBute's] talents go beyond glibly vicious storytelling and extend into thoughtful analyses of a world rotten with original sin." —**Ben Brantley**, *The New York Times*

"LaBute takes us to shadowy places we don't like to talk about, sometimes even to think about . . ." —**Erin McClam**, *Newsday*

WRECKS

"Superb and subversive . . . A masterly attempt to shed light on the ways in which we manufacture our own darkness. It offers us the kind of illumination that Tom Stoppard has called 'what's left of God's purpose when you take away God.'" —**John Lahr**, *The New Yorker*

"[*Wrecks* is a] tasty morsel of a play . . . The profound empathy that has always informed LaBute's work, even at its most stringent, is expressed more directly and urgently than ever here." —**Elysa Gardner**, *USA Today*

"*Wrecks* is bound to be identified by its shock value. But it must also be cherished for the moment-by-moment pleasure of its masterly portraiture. There is not an extraneous syllable in LaBute's enormously moving love story." —**Linda Winer**, *Newsday*

FAT PIG

"The most emotionally engaging and unsettling of Mr. LaBute's plays since *bash* . . . A serious step forward for a playwright who has always been most comfortable with judgmental distance." —**Ben Brantley**, *The New York Times*

"One of Neil LaBute's subtler efforts . . . Demonstrates a warmth and compassion for its characters missing in many of LaBute's previous works [and] balances black humor and social commentary in a . . . beautifully written, hilarious . . . dissection of how societal pressures affect relationships [that] is astute and up-to-the-minute relevant." —**Frank Scheck**, *New York Post*

THE MERCY SEAT

"Though set in the cold, gray light of morning in a downtown loft with inescapable views of the vacuum left by the twin towers, *The Mercy Seat* really occurs in one of those feverish nights of the soul in which men and women lock in vicious sexual combat, as in Strindberg's *Dance of Death* and Edward Albee's *Who's Afraid of Virginia Woolf.*" —**Ben Brantley**, *The New York Times*

"[A] powerful drama . . . LaBute shows a true master's hand in gliding us amid the shoals and reefs of a mined relationship." —**Donald Lyons**, *New York Post*

THE SHAPE OF THINGS

"LaBute . . . continues to probe the fascinating dark side of individualism . . . [His] great gift is to live in and to chronicle that murky area of not-knowing, which mankind spends much of its waking life denying."

—**John Lahr**, *The New Yorker*

"LaBute is the first dramatist since David Mamet and Sam Shepard—since Edward Albee, actually—to mix sympathy and savagery, pathos and power."

—**Donald Lyons**, *New York Post*

"*Shape* . . . is LaBute's thesis on extreme feminine wiles, as well as a disquisition on how far an artist . . . can go in the name of art . . . Like a chiropractor of the soul, LaBute is looking for realignment, listening for a crack."

—**John Istel**, *Elle*

BASH

"The three stories in *bash* are correspondingly all, in different ways, about the power instinct, about the animalistic urge for control. In rendering these narratives, Mr. LaBute shows not only a merciless ear for contemporary speech but also a poet's sense of recurring, slyly graduated imagery . . . darkly engrossing."

—**Ben Brantley**, *The New York Times*

NEIL LABUTE is an award-winning playwright, filmmaker, and screen-writer. His plays include: *bash*, *The Shape of Things*, *The Distance From Here*, *The Mercy Seat*, *Fat Pig* (Olivier Award nominated for Best Comedy), *Some Girl(s)*, *reasons to be pretty* (Tony Award nominated for Best Play), *In A Forest, Dark and Deep*, a new adaptation of *Miss Julie,* and *Reasons to be Happy*. He is also the author of *Seconds of Pleasure*, a collection of short fiction.

Neil LaBute's films include *In the Company of Men* (New York Critics' Circle Award for Best First Feature and the Filmmaker Trophy at the Sundance Film Festival), *Your Friends and Neighbors*, *Nurse Betty*, *Possession*, *The Shape of Things*, *Lakeview Terrace*, *Death at a Funeral*, and *Some Velvet Morning*.

LOVELY HEAD

AND OTHER PLAYS

LOVELY HEAD
A N D   O T H E R   P L A Y S

Neil LaBute

THE OVERLOOK PRESS
NEW YORK, NY

for my man godfrey

*"Her body calculated to a millimeter to suggest
a bud yet guarantee a flower."*
—F. Scott Fitzgerald

CONTENTS

PREFACE

How nice to be back in print.

It's been a few years now since I've had a volume of collected plays appear on bookshelves—and I'm very happy to note that there are still shelves to appear on (at the time of my writing this preface, anyway). Not "virtual" shelves or as a part of an "app" you can download but actual wooden or metal shelves with actual paper books sitting on those shelves. What a lovely feeling and one that periodically threatens to disappear from our lives.

Some people just won't miss books if they go—I'm sure of that for a fact. They're not like Nazis, exactly (they probably don't burn books in their spare time) but they're close enough for my taste. They don't like the *bother* of books: the weight, the size, the smell, the little stacks that gather in the corners of rooms. I love all of that. I live to crack open an old paperback on the street that someone is selling and to breathe in the musk of those pages or to find a forgotten receipt or an inscription or a leaf pressed within the pages. That's wonderful. Occasionally I'll get lucky and find a newspaper clipping from long ago or, better yet, a hand-written or typed note that was saved at some chapter heading and then forgotten—probably a simple book marker that now becomes a gateway to the past in my own hands.

I love books; to write them, to own them, to give and receive them. They are one of the great joys of living as far as I'm concerned. Don't get me wrong, I like watching old re-runs of *The Wild, Wild*

West and eating bad pizza as well, but books are one of the great treasures of my life. My mom introduced me to the pleasures of reading at an early age and I never came back. When I was a kid, going to the public library was almost as good as going to the A & W drive-in or to the movies. Maybe even better. The downtown library in Spokane, Washington, felt so vast and overpowering—I would probably laugh to see its paltry size now as an adult—but even my local branch was a literal world of wonder. We even had book-mobiles in my day. Amazing that those are creatures of the past already and I still feel like a young man (even though I no longer am).

I hope that you—whoever you are—if you're holding this book in your hands and reading this introduction, feel a kindred spirit with books and literature and the pure sense of escape and magic that comes from launching into a world that you know nothing about. If you're an actor and you bring these words to life in class or on a stage, I salute you in a special way because you are brave souls. Being an actor is such a gift and a curse—we love you for it and we judge you for it but most of us just can't do it, no matter how easy you make it look. I, for one, appreciate the pain and euphoria you experience out there under the lights and I will always work to provide you with worthy and worthwhile material. Hopefully you will find some of that enclosed here in this compilation of short works.

Lovely Head, the one-act that lends its name to this volume, was written with an actor in mind but also came about because of a happy encounter I had with a fellow playwright named Marco Calvani. Marco is based in Italy but we met while doing workshops in Barcelona for Sala Beckett, a wonderful fringe theater in that fair city. Marco and I admired each other's work and spoke one day about how rarely we are asked to direct another playwright's work, mostly (I hope) because we are known for writing and directing our own material. Out of that conversation was born a project called AdA (Author directing Author) in which I wrote a play for him to direct and he did the same for me. *Lovely Head* was that play and his was called *Things of This World*, and we subsequently worked on them in Spoleto, Italy, thanks to the hard-working folks at La MaMa Umbria (headed by the indefatigable Mia Yoo) and a terrific group of actors from MIXO (Marco's company in Rome), along with the incredible Urbano Barberini and the exquisite Andrea Ferreol. After finishing at the Spoleto Festival, we subsequently staged both pieces at the Fringe Festival in Madrid and in New York City at the Ellen Stewart Theater (back at La MaMa's home base). In NYC I got to work with the collective brilliant acting minds of Craig Bierko, Gia Crovatin, Larry Pine and Estelle Parsons and I felt that old rush of putting up a show quickly and dangerously, but with the kind of actors that really make you stop and pinch yourself in rehearsal because they're so damn good. AdA was a really special experience and the kind of thing I believe you need to do as a long-time competitor in these theatrical sweepstakes known as a "career": no matter how it all turns out, you need to keep trying new things.

I should also say that the title of this play was too clever for me to have come up with it on my own—my thanks goes to the members of the musical group called Goldfrapp, whose song I ripped it off from. It was meant as a tribute to their great and ethereal work (go listen to *Felt Mountain* if you haven't heard it already).

All of these other plays have either made their debut or at least played at some venue in New York City (with the exception of *Over the River and Through the Woods*, which will make its New York debut later this year). A few started on the West Coast, one as a short film and two of them, as you will see, are monologues (one of them first performed by the actress Alice Eve and the other one first performed by this author—I'll leave it to you to sort out which one is which).

All of them were fun to write, to work on and/or to watch in performance. I've been so lucky to constantly have great actors to elevate my material up on stage. I hope this trend continues forever —believe me, you know the difference when you see it.

A quick word about the play *Strange Fruit*, which was written for a show called *Standing On Ceremony* and was a collection of short plays defending gay marriage. I was asked by a gifted producer named Joan Stein (who passed away just last year) if I would be interested in writing something and my automatic answer was "yes." I'm always interested in the theater, whatever the venue, whatever the time and whatever the reason. I love it. That said, I did it as much for her as anything; we had worked together years ago on the play *bash* in Los Angeles and since then I had know her as a lover of life and a crusader for theater and basic human rights. Joan was the real deal, a person who looked you straight in the eye and told you the truth. She will be missed.

Thank you—whomever you are—for reading this, for putting up with me and for continuing to read or perform or despise or love or dismiss or praise my work. Thank you for coming back and trying it once again—I feel the same way you do about me: "sometimes he's good, sometimes he's bad, but at least the guy keeps swinging for the fences." I hope that all of you in this profession, from onlooker to critic to artist, keep doing that very same thing.

Neil LaBute
January 2013

LOVELY HEAD

Lovely Head had its American premiere at La MaMa in New York City in September 2012. It was directed by Marco Calvani.

MAN   Larry Pine
GIRL   Gia Crovatin

Silence. Darkness.

Lights up on a living room—nice but it has an antiseptic feel to it somehow, as if the whole thing is a rental or something. It isn't, but it has that look.

MAN seated on a couch, staring at a television. Some kind of noise coming out of it, probably an infomercial. Maybe sports.

After a moment, he gets up and looks out the window, then glances at his watch. Tries to sit again but goes to make a water with ice in the adjoining kitchen. As he does it, the doorbell rings and he spills the drink.

MAN   . . . coming! I'm coming!!

He quickly grabs a roll of paper towels and pulls off a long piece, trying to mop up the mess. He ends up in a tangle and shakes it off. He moves the sopping pile into the sink and wipes his hands, moving toward the door at a trot. He side-steps and turns off the TV and snaps on the stereo. He checks himself in a mirror and goes to the door. Stops, takes a couple deep breaths, then opens it.

A GIRL *stands near the threshold, looking off. She is a dazzler— gorgeous hair, shortish skirt, heels. Sunglasses cover her eyes. Like Lolita working for Avon.*

She turns slowly and looks at him, then saunters past.

The MAN *steps aside to let her in, then waves to someone outside before closing the door behind himself. A moment between them.*

GIRL . . . took you long enough.

MAN Sorry, I was . . . sorry.

GIRL It's your money.

MAN No, I know that, I realize that it's . . . anyway, forgive me. (*Beat.*) . . . I spilled something.

GIRL I get that a lot.

MAN Really?

GIRL No, it's a joke. Don't ya get it?

MAN Ummmmmmm . . . no, actually. I don't.

GIRL Forget it.

MAN No, please, I'd . . . what're you saying? I just didn't follow . . . your . . .

GIRL Guys. Spilling stuff. *On* me. (*Beat.*) Does that help?

MAN Oh. (*Gets it.*) *Ohhhhhhh*, right . . . got it.

GIRL Good.

MAN I get it *now*. Yes.

GIRL Great.

MAN That's . . . very *candid*. As always.

GIRL Yep.

MAN Quite funny, really. That's a good one . . .

GIRL Uh-huh. (*Beat.*) So?

MAN Right! So, so, so. Should we . . . do you wanna sit, or . . . ?

GIRL Up to you.

MAN Let's sit. I'd like that. Yes. (*Beat.*) We usually sit, so we should
. . . ummmm . . .

GIRL Ok, then. Let's sit.

The MAN *indicates the couch and they move over to sit on it.* GIRL
checks her own watch. Pushes her glasses up onto her forehead.

MAN Can I get you anything?

GIRL Ummm . . . should we maybe, you know?

MAN What?

GIRL You-know.

MAN No. I'm . . . ?

GIRL You are a funny one . . . (*Beat.*) Business?

MAN Ahhh, God, sorry, yes! Of course. We need to take care of . . .
sure. That's . . .

GIRL Yeah.

MAN Forgive me. There we go, all set. (*Beat.*) I did the cash how you
like it, with the twenties in one bunch and then the tens and fives
in their own . . . little . . . just how you showed me. The way you
like it.

He points to an envelope on the end table. The GIRL *looks at it,
then reaches over and gathers it up. Checks inside it. Tosses it into
her bag.*

GIRL Cool. Thanks.

MAN Not a problem.

GIRL 'ppreciate it.

MAN Absolutely.

GIRL So?

MAN Yes. So. (*Beat.*) Would you like a drink or anything? Maybe some . . . ?

GIRL Water'd be good. I'd take a water if you got it.

MAN Sure. Of *course* I've got water . . .

GIRL Great.

MAN . . . I mean, I've *definitely* got that.

The GIRL *nods and so does the* MAN. *She continues to wait.*

GIRL . . . then . . . how about getting me some?

He jumps up and practically runs over to the fridge. He slips on the puddle that's still there and drops to the floor, disappearing for a moment.

GIRL Hey! You alright?!

MAN I'm ok, absolutely . . . just caught a slick spot here. Hold on . . .

The MAN *gets to his feet, straightens himself out. Smiles as he tries to regain some dignity. Opens the door to the fridge.*

GIRL Took quite a spill there . . .

MAN Right! (*Laughs.*) You must get that all the time . . .

GIRL What?

MAN *Spills*? (*Beat.*) Remember, from a little bit ago? You said the . . . the . . .

GIRL I was joking.

MAN Sure, but . . . I mean, so am *I*. It's a joke.

GIRL Well, jokes should be *amusing* . . .

MAN Sorry, I was . . . trying . . . to be . . .

GIRL Can I have that water?

MAN Of course. Yes. (*Looks in fridge.*) Ahhh, do you like . . . ?
I have Dasani or Fiji. You can have either.

GIRL Doesn't matter. They both have weird names, so it doesn't
matter.

MAN Oh. Well . . . actually, there's a pretty big difference.

GIRL Yeah?

MAN Uh-huh. One is just, you know, water. It was all purified and
everything, but . . . Fiji's much better. *Spring* water, from the
source and all that. Delicious.

GIRL It's *water*.

MAN Right, I know, but . . . it comes out of an *aquifer* that's deep in
the side of the . . . doesn't matter. It's just better.

GIRL How can it be delicious?

MAN I dunno. It really is, though.

GIRL Water doesn't have any taste.

MAN I know that, I know, but . . . it's still . . .

GIRL Doesn't something have to have a taste for it to be delicious?
I mean, I'm not like a *chef* or anything, but . . .

MAN No, right, I know what you're saying but you really can tell . . .
it's amazing how different two things can be, two *like* things and
yet *so* different . . . (*Beat.*) Or you can have tap. It's up to you.

GIRL Well . . . which one do you usually give me? I mean, when you
don't ask and just put a glass down in front of me . . . which one is
that?

MAN Fiji. Unless I don't have it, but mostly that when I do. Usually
it's the Fiji.

GIRL Ummmm . . . fine. I'll take Fiji then.

MAN Great! I think you'll really like it . . .

GIRL Thanks. (*Checks her phone.*) Do you mind?

MAN Ahhhhh, I'd prefer you didn't . . .

GIRL But I can, right? *Please*?

MAN . . . sure. But just . . . okay . . . even though I'd rather that you didn't. It's kind of rude . . . when you're visiting . . . someone . . .

The GIRL *isn't listening. She is texting.* MAN *grabs a bottle of Fiji out of the fridge and grabs a small plate from the rack.*

MAN Here you go. (*Points.*) You can use this for a coaster . . . it's a *plate*, but . . .

GIRL I *know*. I can *see* that.

He hurries back over to the couch. Puts a small plate down in front of her. Stands.

GIRL Are you gonna sit?

MAN Oh, sure.

GIRL I like it better when you sit. It makes me nervous when you don't . . .

MAN I'm sorry. Of course, I'm happy to.

The MAN *sits down, watching the* GIRL *finish reading and then sending yet another text. She finishes and puts her phone down. Smiles over at him.*

GIRL . . . you always say that. With the plate thingie. Why do you do that?

MAN Because I'm . . . just so you'll know.

GIRL Do you think I'm retarded or something? I can remember things . . . things like that, anyway. To use the plate for a coaster. I mean, seriously. Duh.

MAN No, I know you can . . . I mean, why do you ask if you can text when you're here? As many times as you've been here, you still always ask me permission . . .

The GIRL *looks over at him. Shrugs.*

GIRL Because I'm *polite*, I guess. Whatever. Doesn't matter.

MAN Yes, but it's interesting . . . you know I don't want you to, I always ask you *not* to . . . but you still do it.

GIRL So?

MAN So . . . I'm just saying, if we're gonna ask questions . . . we could probably start with that one!

GIRL Right . . . (*Smiles.*) And is that what you wanna do with our time? Ask questions?

MAN . . . no.

GIRL 'Kay. Good.

The GIRL *takes a sip from the water. Then another.*

GIRL Mmmmmm. That *is* tasty . . . mmmmmmmmm!

MAN See? Told you.

GIRL I'm kidding.

MAN Oh. Another *joke*, huh?

GIRL Yeah. One of the *amusing* kind . . .

MAN Right.

GIRL I can't really tell the difference with the water. Sorry.

MAN You can't?

GIRL Uh-uh.

MAN It's the best around—I've heard lots of people say that about Fiji. (*Beat.*) *Lots*.

The GIRL opens her eyes wide and shakes her hands in the air as if to say: "Wow, that's amazing!"

GIRL Then maybe you should have them over for a *party* or something. A water party and you can all talk about it. You can meet up at the *aquifer* with your little aqua friends and just . . . like . . . compare the different brands and shit. Sounds fun!

MAN . . . that's another joke, isn't it? You're just . . . you're making fun of me now.

GIRL Yeah. Kind of.

MAN Okay. Well, I just wanted you to have the best one. That's all.

GIRL Fine. (*Softening.*) Thank you . . .

MAN It's alright.

GIRL No, that's sweet, I guess. Thanks.

MAN Not a problem.

GIRL . . . why do you even have the other kind?

MAN Sorry?

GIRL Of water. The kind that you don't really recommend? If this type is *so* good, why do you keep the other one around?

MAN . . . ummmmmmm . . . just for . . .

GIRL I'm curious.

MAN It's . . . for, you know. (*Beat.*) Guests.

GIRL Oh. *Nice*.

MAN No, I don't mean for, like, *you* . . . but if somebody happens to stop over, or if one of the lawn guys—the people that cut my grass and stuff—if one of them wanted a drink . . . I'd probably give 'em that brand.

GIRL Is it cheaper?

MAN   No, it's . . . well, yeah. It usually is.

GIRL   And is that why?

MAN   Why, what?

GIRL   Why you'd give it to them.

MAN   . . . I . . . suppose . . .

GIRL   Because you don't wanna waste it. The other kind, the Fiji one.

MAN   No, I don't think *that's* why . . .

GIRL   Then what?

MAN   Just in case, I guess! I keep it on hand for just in case I run out of the other—*but* sometimes I'll give it out to people who're . . . you know . . . *others* . . . who . . .

GIRL   . . . who might not deserve the good stuff. Right?

MAN   . . . yes. That's probably true.

GIRL   Huh. (*Beat.*) That's kinda fucked up, don't you think?

The MAN *nods but doesn't answer her. He glances at his watch, then back at the* GIRL. *She smiles.*

GIRL   Oh, I'm sorry . . . am I cutting into your hour?

MAN   No, no, I just lost track of . . . the . . .

GIRL   . . . uh-huh. *Sure.*

MAN   I really did! I have this . . . appointment later today, so . . . I was . . . checking . . .

GIRL   Yeah, me too. I've got one right after I'm done here.

MAN   What?

GIRL   An "appointment." Duh. A *rendezvous*.

MAN   Oh. *Ohhhhhhh*, right. Got it.

GIRL   Fine. (*Beat.*) So?

MAN   That's . . . .you always say that. "So?" It really unnerves me, I gotta tell you. It does. Hearing that all the time.

GIRL   What?

MAN When you say that. "So."

GIRL I'm sorry! It's a habit, I guess . . .

MAN Really?

GIRL Uh-huh.

MAN Why's that? I mean, how'd it become a habit, do you think? Just . . . from you . . . from saying it so often? *Or* . . . ?

GIRL God, you ask a *lot* of questions . . .

MAN Sorry. Is that a problem?

GIRL There's another one . . .

MAN I just . . . what's so *bad* about questions?

GIRL Nothing. Unless you always ask them? And then your voice always does that thing? Where it raises up at the end? And then it's just really, really annoying?

The GIRL *smiles at him innocently, then takes a drink.*

GIRL Ummmmmm, that's *delicious*! What is this?

MAN Funny. That's very cute . . .

GIRL That's my specialty. Cute. The *cute* girl-next-door. (*Beat.*) And golden showers, but that's another story . . . (*Does a rim shot.*) Ba-*da*-bah!

MAN Right, right. O-kay.

GIRL Don't you think that's true . . . don't you find me at all cute? Hmmmm?

MAN Of course I do . . . you *know* I do.

GIRL I'm glad. That makes me happy. Honestly.

MAN Good. (*Beat.*) . . . Is the music alright?

GIRL Yeah, it's fine.

MAN Sure?

GIRL Very nice. I'm glad you took my advice.

MAN It's a good album. Crazy name, but it's nice stuff. "Gold*frapp*."

(*Beat.*) Thanks . . .

GIRL Any time. As long as you pay for a *full* session, of course . . .

MAN . . . (*Beat.*) You know what? You make a *lot* of those . . .

ummmmmm . . .

GIRL What?

MAN Nothing. It's no big deal.

GIRL No, what?

MAN You know, "hooker" jokes . . . does that help or whatever?

If . . . you . . . do that?

GIRL Help what?

MAN I dunno. Help make you—doesn't matter.

GIRL Go on, say it . . . (*Beat.*) And nobody uses the word "hooker"

any more, by the way! *No* one. Old dudes, college kids, not any

body. Just so you know . . .

MAN *Fine*. I was just . . . trying to . . . be . . .

GIRL Look, I tell jokes—I mean, they're not even jokes! I just say shit,

goofy shit sometimes—and I do it because I'm funny . . . not to

ease my pain or any ridiculous crap like that. Ok? I mean, God . . .

MAN I didn't mean anything by it. I only . . .

GIRL This really isn't gonna work if it always turns into some kind of

stupid . . . *therapy* deal . . . every time we see each other!

MAN I wasn't doing that! Honestly.

GIRL Well, that's what it seems like—like you feel guilty about some-

thing, or, like . . . want *me* to feel guilty or, or . . . whatever.

MAN Sorry. (*Beat.*) No.

GIRL I know you keep looking for that "heart of gold" shit but I'm

here because you pay me, alright? *Over*-pay me, actually, and

that is the reason I come back here, even give you the time of

day! Now, can you *handle* that or do we have a problem?

MAN . . . no, no, I . . . understand.

GIRL You do?

MAN Yes. Not, like, in the greater *scheme* of things but . . . yes. I get it. I get *that*. I get the "quit asking your stupid shit" part of all this, so . . . uh-huh. I do.

GIRL Good. (*Laughs.*) See, now *that* was funny! Nice one . . .

The GIRL *waits a minute, then scoots closer to the* MAN.

GIRL So?

MAN See? You did it again.

GIRL Well, what would *you* say? If you were me, I mean? Seriously, what?

MAN . . . I dunno.

GIRL No, go ahead . . . tell me.

MAN I'd . . . I'm really not sure. I can't do that sort of thing.

GIRL Do what?

MAN Imagine what it'd be like to be you. (*Beat.*) To do what you *do* . . . not just because of the job, but . . . you know. Due to . . . *our* . . . thingie. Situation.

GIRL I see.

MAN I don't mean anything by that, I really, really don't . . . I just can't. It's like a lot of things—you can't *know* what it's like to do something until you *do* it . . .

GIRL Well, I suppose that's true. Like riding a bike. Or scuba diving . . .

MAN . . . yeah. Like that. Except . . . I mean . . .

GIRL What?

MAN You know.

GIRL No, what?

MAN Except that . . . you . . . just forget it.

GIRL Except in scuba diving you wouldn't suck on anybody's cock, is that what you mean?

MAN . . . I wasn't going to say that.

GIRL No, but that's what you meant, isn't it? It's what you were thinking?

MAN Sort of. Yes.

GIRL Well, that's true . . . I mean, unless it was connected to an air tank. A cock, I mean. Or had, like, some *oxygen* trapped inside of it . . . then you would. Right? I mean . . . some person in general would. (*Beat.*) Not you, though. Even then you wouldn't. *You* in particular, I mean.

MAN . . . no. I don't think so.

GIRL I mean, *I* would and that's why I'd live—in a situation like that, where if a cock made the difference between me living and dying . . . I'd get myself busy down there—but obviously you would not. You'd rather *drown* than do that, wouldn't you? To suck on some other guy's cock, even if by the act of sucking you'd be spared. Hmmmm?

MAN . . . I guess so . . .

GIRL Or even your own cock, for that matter. If you could—anatomically, I'm saying—if you could do that you wouldn't, would you? Not even to save yourself. (*Beat.*) I don't think you'd touch that thing with a *ten-foot pole*, even if that was the only difference between you living and dying. *Isn't* that true?

MAN . . . I dunno . . . I'd probably . . . just . . .

GIRL No, I do. I *do* know. I know *exactly* what you think you'd do—or not do—in that situation. You-would-die. Am I right?

MAN Probably! I mean, if you put it *that* way, then yes. I would die. (*Beat.*) I'm not even very comfortable with that *word*, so . . . you know . . . I wouldn't . . .

GIRL Right . . . but you don't mind it when *I* use it, do you? Talk dirty like that, I mean. You don't hate it when *I* say "cock" or, like, "cum" or whatever . . . do you? I mean, I don't recall you ever stopping me. So.

MAN . . . no. It's . . . I don't *love* it, but, you know. I'm okay with it. (*Beat.*) Not in a *sexual* way—at all—but you're an adult.

GIRL I'll bet. (*Beat.*) And that's bullshit, by the way. You and the cock thing, because if you were dying, or about to, and that was the difference between being alive or not, I bet you'd *suck* your little brains out. You *absolutely* would. (*Makes noises.*)

MAN No, I wouldn't. Uh-uh. No.

GIRL Oh yeah, sure . . . *liar.*

MAN I really wouldn't! I *promise* you . . . I'm not able to—even if it did save me, as you say—I can't even *imagine* doing that! I *really* really can't.

GIRL Huh. Well . . . that just makes you fucking stupid, then. And an idiot.

MAN Maybe so—at least that's what you think—but I know myself. I could *never* do that. Put someone's *thing* in my mouth. Another man's *penis*? No, not ever. (*Beat.*) NO.

GIRL . . . hmm. Aren't we picky?

They sit in silence for a moment, not moving. They both check their watches. Looking around the room.

GIRL What *other* way is there to put it, by the way? The "scuba" analogy?

MAN Sorry?

GIRL You said "if you put it *that* way," but I can't think of any other way *to* put it. There's only one way to put a thing like that . . . isn't there? And that's in your mouth. (*Grins.*) I'm *joking.*

MAN I know . . . (*Beat.*) I do sometimes get 'em! Your jokes.

GIRL Well, that's good. (*Checks phone.*) So?

MAN What? I'm lost . . . I don't know what you're asking me here. I'm . . . just . . .

GIRL . . . not asking, *saying*. Saying that all that shit you just said was basically another way to tell me that you can't understand what I'm doing with my life. Right? To get us onto a subject that you know pisses me off but you just can't seem to stop yourself from talking about it . . . from *harping* on it . . .

MAN Ummm, I think you started this, actually.

GIRL . . . no . . . *you're* the one who . . .

MAN Yes . . . with the scuba thing and all, yeah. You did.

GIRL No, uh-uh, you got on the whole topic of "I can't imagine what it'd be like to be you" shit! *You* said that!!

MAN I know, but . . . that was because you . . .

GIRL . . . *you* started it!

MAN No, I was just . . . trying to . . .

GIRL You did, you *totally* did!

MAN Fine. I'm sorry! It's my fault. Okay?

GIRL Doesn't matter.

MAN I didn't mean to make you . . . sorry.

GIRL It-doesn't-matter. (*Beat.*) So?

MAN Yeah, "so." We should just . . . yes.

GIRL Uh-huh. If we're gonna do something. (*Beat.*) You wanna see my pussy?

MAN I'm . . . do you have to talk that way?

GIRL What? Just for a second. Nobody'd know.

MAN I just wish you'd—*please* don't say that. Can we just keep doing *this*? Is that ok?

GIRL If you wanna.

MAN I do. I like this.

GIRL Then go for it. Same as usual. (*Checking her watch.*) You got, about, forty minutes left.

MAN Great. That's . . . good. I'm glad.

GIRL Yep.

The MAN *sits back, takes a moment. The* GIRL *leans over and checks her phone again. Sends another text as she takes one more sip of her water. She looks around.*

GIRL Do you have a coaster or can I just use this *plate*? (*Smiles.*) Just wanna lighten things up a touch . . .

MAN Right, right! No problem.

GIRL You're always so tense.

MAN I know. Can't help it.

GIRL Well, it makes me jumpy, so . . .

MAN I understand.

GIRL Then stop.

MAN I'm trying, I really am. It's not easy.

GIRL Try harder, then. (*Beat.*) People can do whatever they need to do, that's a fact. If they want to. It's that "mind-over-matter" shit, that's what it is . . .

MAN True. I'll . . . do my best . . .

GIRL You do that. And *soon*, 'kay?

He smiles and tries to settle back into the couch. She rearranges herself and they look at each other.

MAN Promise! I'll look into it . . . (*Laughs.*) Anyway, I just like to spend a minute or two chatting when we can . . . we never get that much

time to just, you know, talk or that type of thing. Really *speak* to
each other . . . we always seem to get *so* caught up . . . in . . .

GIRL . . . you should buy another hour, then . . .

MAN Well, maybe you could gimme a break on the price! A deal of
some sort . . .

GIRL I don't think you get how this works.

MAN . . . I'm joking . . .

GIRL Oh, right. One of those kind that aren't funny . . .

MAN Exactly! (*Smiles.*) Honestly, though . . . couldn't we, I dunno,
get lunch or something? Meet up at a park or maybe . . . I'm just
talking about an *afternoon* here! That type of thing.

GIRL And what do you think my answer's gonna be to that? Huh?

MAN Absolutely not. No chance in hell. (*Beat.*) Something like that?

GIRL You got it! (*Looks around.*) Hey, you wanna turn the air on . . .
or a fan or something? (*Beat.*) Doesn't matter to me but it feels
kinda stuffy in here . . . so maybe . . .

MAN No, wait, *listen* to me, please. Why can't we meet up some
afternoon? (*Beat.*) Are you listening to me? *Jennifer*?

The GIRL *stops suddenly and jumps to her feet, angry.*

GIRL Don't do that! Ok?!! Do *not*, or I am out the door and I'll have
that big dude out front—the guy you always wave to? Manny—
I will have him come in here and put his *foot* up your ass!! You got
that?!!! Up-your-ass . . . and he's got a *huge* fucking foot!! I am
not playing around with you anymore about this!! Not *one* more
time!! YOU HEAR ME?!!

MAN . . . *please* . . . I was just . . .

GIRL DO YOU?!!!

MAN Yes. I understand.

GIRL Good . . . because that's the *last* time you are gonna pull a fucking trick like that! You got that?! Huh?!!

MAN Sorry. I'm sorry . . . I just wanted to get your *attention*, but I wasn't . . .

GIRL You can call me "Amber" or "little girl" or whatever the hell you'd like, but do not *ever* use that name again. Don't use my name or, or, like, bring up where I'm from or any of that shit, because that's *none* of your fucking *business*! Ok?!!

MAN Ok. I can see that.

GIRL You better. You had better "see" and get it right the next time or I'm out of this shithole! (*Beat.*) God!! You're so . . . fuck, that pisses me off!!

MAN I didn't mean to make you mad.

GIRL No?!

MAN Of course not.

GIRL Really?! How many times have you said my name before, huh? My *real* name?!

MAN . . . a . . . couple . . .

She shakes her head angrily and holds up some fingers.

GIRL How-many?

MAN I don't know! (*Beat.*) Three, maybe? Three times . . . ?

GIRL And how'd I feel about that? Each of those times, *how* did I react?

MAN You didn't seem—you weren't too crazy about it.

GIRL Exactly! I told you to *never* do it again and so you stop and I come back here and it's all going fine until you try to *lull* me into some little *comfort zone* and then you try to *slip* it in again . . . like maybe *this* time she won't notice! I mean, *please*! Just listen to

what I'm saying here, ok?! Don't-use-my-fucking-name again!!!
Seems pretty simple . . .

MAN I won't. I promise.

GIRL Yeah well, excuse me for being skeptical, but your *promises*
seem to be written with invisible ink on Houdini's ass!!

MAN I really will not do it again. *Amber.*

GIRL . . . great . . .

MAN I'm sorry. Honestly.

GIRL Fine. (*Beat.*) Shit, this whole thing has given me a headache.
Some kind of ache, right here. (*Points.*) You got aspirin?

MAN I do, yes. Well, Tylenol . . . is that ok?

The MAN *stands to go find a bottle in a nearby cabinet.*

MAN Or Advil. I have both. Your choice . . .

GIRL What've you got, *two* choices for everything? It's fucking
aspirin!!

MAN Sorry, I just try to be . . . doesn't matter. I'll get you some.

He scurries over to another set of cabinets and searches around.

GIRL You wanna grab me four or so?

MAN Ummmmmm . . . that's a lot.

GIRL Don't act like my *dad*, alright? (*Beat.*) Just get the . . . pills . . .

MAN Fine. It's your body . . .

GIRL That's right. That is *exactly* right . . . it's mine and I'll do
whatever the hell I want with it, including taking a *therapeutic*
dose of painkillers when I need it!

MAN I'll grab you four . . .

GIRL Thank you.

The MAN *heads for the kitchen and keeps looking. He approaches that slick spot again and goes down to one knee—just catching himself. The* GIRL *laughs at this.*

MAN Damnit!

GIRL Be careful . . . God, you are such a fucking *doofus* sometimes . . . seriously.

MAN It's slick over here, that's all!

GIRL Well, you did it last time . . . you can't remember that for, like, *twenty* seconds? That it's slippery there? Duh.

MAN I can, yes, of course I can . . . I just didn't, so . . . I, I fell.

He bends over for a moment, brushing himself clean and picking lint off his trousers.

GIRL That's dumb. Doesn't make any sense . . .

MAN It's . . . (*Waves it off.*) Nothing. Lemme just get the pills from the . . . I have a little first-aid thing here. (*Searching around.*) Where the hell is the . . . I have a woman who comes in and cleans and she . . .

The MAN *reaches into a cabinet and pulls out a box that is stuffed with medical goodies—bandages, iodine, the works. He pulls out a bottle and counts out four pills.*

He returns to the GIRL *and drops the pills into her hand.*

She gobbles them down, then chases it with a sip of her water. The MAN *sits after this.*

GIRL . . . thanks. That's better.

MAN Really? They're working already?

GIRL I was being metaphorical. Jesus, what do you think?

MAN I . . . you never know. I mean, with the way medicine is these days.

GIRL Come on! Nothing works *that* fast . . .

MAN I *know*, but . . . I was just being a little bit courteous. Alright? Showing a touch of interest in you . . .

GIRL Oh.

MAN *Sorry*.

GIRL No, that's cool . . . I guess.

MAN They'll work in a minute or two.

GIRL I know, I'm not stupid . . .

MAN Alright, alright.

They both sit back and wait for a moment—staring off into space and contemplating. Silence. After a moment, the GIRL *looks at the* MAN *and puts her legs in his lap.*

GIRL And don't think I'm stopping the clock for this, ok?

MAN . . . no, I didn't *figure* you would . . .

GIRL . . . alright then. (*Beat.*) Just so we're on the same page.

MAN We are.

GIRL Great.

They sit in silence. The GIRL *looking around the room.*

The MAN *sits and watches her. She notices and finally says something:*

GIRL . . . it's weird when you stare at me like that. I'm not being mean, but . . .

MAN I'm sorry!

GIRL It's alright. I'm just saying.

MAN I'll stop.

GIRL It doesn't make me mad or that sort of thing . . . it's just weird. That's all.

MAN I don't mean to, it's just . . . you're . . .

GIRL I know.

MAN It's hard not to. (*Beat.*) I can't help but see you back when things were . . . you know. Before.

He steals another glance at her. She notices but doesn't say anything this time around.

She checks her phone again. Texts while she says:

GIRL I get it and I'm not saying that you have to stop or anything . . . just . . .

MAN Thank you.

GIRL Welcome.

MAN . . . I'm . . .

GIRL . . . it's unusual, that's all. Not what I'm used to.

MAN I suppose that's true . . .

GIRL Most guys, they're so busy trying to get my panties down or their belts off, they don't take a lot of time to look at my face. Not that much, anyway. I mean . . . after that first minute. Right when they open the door—check to make sure that none of their neighbors are watching or whatever—then they'll glance at me, to make certain that I'm pretty enough or the kind of girl they imagined—

young, that seems to be what most men want, someone young who still wants them—after that little second, though, they couldn't care less who I am . . . all they wanna see is my ass or tits or, you know . . . to lay back and close their eyes. (*Beat.*) So it's strange when you do that. Stare over at me. It is . . .

MAN I can't help it. Not really.

GIRL I get it. (*Beat.*) So?

MAN You don't have to say that . . .

GIRL Yeah, I do.

MAN No you don't, you really don't have to.

GIRL Time is ticking away here . . .

MAN I know, but . . . all I'm saying is, we don't have to do anything, you know that, there is never a need for us to . . . I just wanna *talk* to you, that's all. I want to speak with you and hear your voice, see if . . . I dunno, if you need anything or if I can be of some . . . what-ever . . . *service*. Can I pass along a message . . . or maybe just . . . ?

GIRL . . . what? "Maybe just" what?

MAN . . . you know.

GIRL Yeah, I do. I do know but I wanna hear you say it. (*Beat.*) Go for it.

MAN I'm . . . just asking . . .

GIRL I would like to hear you say it one more time, to see that you've got the balls to do that, to repeat it *once* more even when I've asked you, like, a *million* times not to. Over and over. So, go ahead . . .

MAN That's alright. Forget it.

GIRL No, *do* it. Say it!

MAN I said last time that I wouldn't, so . . .

GIRL But you *want* to! You *wanna* do it, so go on then. Say it. Seriously, show me that you've got at least *that* much inside . . . Go-on.

MAN Fine. (*Beat.*) Look . . . I want to get you, you know, out of here, out of this . . . *life* . . . that you're . . . and get you back in school, or, or, or I'm not sure! God, just into some . . . other . . .

GIRL . . . yeah? *What?*

MAN I dunno!! *Out*, that's all, start over or maybe go back home, something . . .

GIRL Huh.

MAN We'd pay for everything and it could be—I'm not gonna make up stories . . . it would be hard but we could do it—it's a thing that I can see . . . working out . . . I'm just saying that I'd like to do that! For you.

GIRL You wanna save me, right?

MAN No! No, not "save," but . . . just . . .

GIRL Say it. Say the words.

MAN . . . it's not about "saving" you . . .

GIRL You-want-to-save-me, so say it then.

MAN Alright! I do, yes! If that means *helping* you then yes, I wanna *help* you . . . Amber.

GIRL Because why? Because you feel bad?

MAN I do . . . yeah. I feel bad.

GIRL For who? *Me?*

MAN Yes . . . for you, and not just you but for anybody who would find themselves in a . . . *spot* like this. This, this place.

GIRL I didn't wake up here, you know. Like, up from some dream and I'm all bound and in a trunk headed to *Saudi Arabia* . . . I do it 'cause I *want* to. I *like* it. (*Beat.*) I do.

MAN No, come on . . . that's . . . (*Beat.*) You can't.

GIRL What the fuck do you mean?

MAN I'm saying you can do it . . . but *like* it? *Want* to do it? How's that even possible?

GIRL Wow . . . you got in, like, three questions in a row that time. That's a record . . .

MAN Come on, please! This is . . . very . . . !

GIRL No, you come on!! *Who* the fuck are you to talk to me like that? Anything like that?

MAN . . . you know who I am . . .

GIRL No, I don't. I really don't.

MAN I'm your . . . come on, I don't wanna do *this*. Play this game.

GIRL Say it! Say it! SAY IT!!

MAN Ok, fine! I'm *me*. Gary, your uncle . . . that's who I am. I am your Uncle Gary and I want to help you, Jenny . . .

GIRL Fuck it, I'm outta here! You *blew* it!!

MAN No, listen to me! Listen! Stop!!

GIRL NO!! (*On her feet now.*) I TOLD YOU!!

MAN Wait . . . STOP!! Jennifer!!

GIRL DON'T CALL ME THAT!! I'M NOT "JENNIFER!" SHE'S DEAD, JENNIFER IS DEAD AND I DON'T WANNA HEAR THAT FUCKING NAME EVER AGAIN!

MAN Alright, fine . . . I didn't mean to . . .

GIRL My family killed her—do you get that?!! She's not here! She's gone! (*Beat.*) FUCK! SHIT!! I'm so fucking sick of your . . . why do you *do* this?! Huh?! Book me for these *creepy* . . . do you know what my dad would do if he knew the truth about all of this? *Do* you?!

MAN . . . yes.

GIRL . . . what he'd do if he found out that you know what I am and how I'm doing it *and* that you call me, that you *actually* ring up and book me to come over to your . . . do an outcall with you at least, what? Once a week? I mean, at *least* that often . . . do you have *any* idea?!! Huh?!!

MAN . . . but that's because . . . that is *because* I'm . . .

GIRL He would cut your balls off!! Right off your fucking body!! YOU *KNOW* THAT!! YOU *KNOW* HE WOULD!!

MAN I do it so I can keep an eye on you . . . this is for *you*!!

GIRL I'll bet.

MAN . . . what're you saying?

GIRL I'm saying *exactly* what I mean.

MAN *What*?

GIRL You know . . . come on . . . "Uncle" Gary.

MAN I do this . . . "Amber" . . . so that at least somebody in the family knows you're alive! From the very first you knew that. You've allowed me to say that I've seen you, that you're ok and not off in some *ditch* or, or at a . . . meth house, or . . .

She laughs at this one. He doesn't know much, this guy.

GIRL You mean *crack* house! Jesus, you're such a classic. There's no such thing as that, a "meth house." You mean "meth lab?"

MAN Yes! Yes there is! I've watched it on the television, a place where they make, you know . . . meth. (*Beat.*) Is that a "meth *lab*?"

GIRL Yeah! And why would *I* be there? Huh? I'm not a chemist.

MAN Right, but you could be . . . you know!! One of those naked girls they use to stir up the . . . all the . . . I've *seen* it in movies!!

She laughs again.

GIRL Yep. That could've been me . . .

MAN You *know* what I'm saying! Shit! (*Looking over at her.*) Sorry, I don't swear often, as you know, but this whole . . . thing . . . is just . . . it flusters me!! I'm . . . I'm . . .

GIRL I know. (*Beat.*) I get that.

MAN I haven't told the *truth* to anyone—and I thought that you appreci-
ated that, that I was winning your trust with it—because I understand
the situation. Both sides. You have legitimate . . . things . . . that you
have reacted to and . . . but he's my brother . . . your dad is, he's my
brother and I'm here watching over you as best I can—yes, it might
be unorthodox, what I've done, *yes*—but I'm *trying*. I am trying here.
Not to scare you off and have you disappear. Not to let them lose
hope. I don't know what to do! Most days it tears me up inside, I can
feel my guts twisting around because of a secret that I have and
I don't want it . . . I don't want to carry this around, all of this stuff
I know about you, but I do! I pay you money . . . money that I do not
necessarily have and, and I'll sit here afterwards and I'll just . . . cry,
like when you say you're off to another one of your meetings, I'll just
start *weeping* because I can't stop it . . . I can't tell anyone, so I just
. . . yeah. I cry. (*Beat.*) Because I care about you "Amber," I really do.
You've made it clear what you'll do if I tell your dad anything real
about you and so I'd rather lie . . . I'd rather be doing this . . . than
having no idea if you are alive or dead. (*Beat.*) So I guess we'll just
keep on following the . . . I would buy every day, every *hour* with you
if I had the money, if I could afford that, to keep you off the streets!
But I can't, and it makes me sick that I can't but that's just the way it
is right now. "Amber." (*Beat.*) . . . do I have to keep using that stupid
name? It's *so* silly . . . I mean, even when we're . . . just . . . here?

GIRL . . . yes. (*Tears in her eyes.*) You do. Yes.

MAN Fine. "Amber." (*Beat.*) I guess you should go now, or . . .
whatever. I'm sorry to make this *so* . . . you know. *Dramatic.*

A frozen moment for both of them. They're unsure how to go on now.

GIRL . . . ok. (*Checking her phone.*) We still have twenty minutes.

MAN I know, but . . . I'm . . .

GIRL I mean, "better here than there" . . . right? Isn't that what you always say?

MAN Usually. Something stupid like that.

GIRL Ha! It's only *kinda* stupid. (*Beat.*) You're not so bad, I guess . . . for an "uncle."

MAN Thanks. Thank you.

GIRL Welcome.

They sit back together on the couch. Closer now than they were before. After a moment, she yawns. Twice, even.

MAN Tired?

GIRL Kinda. Late night.

MAN I'm not asking . . .

GIRL Probably for the best. (*Smiling.*) See? You're learning.

MAN Yep.

GIRL I'm just gonna rest a minute, ok?

MAN Sure.

GIRL I got a busy day, so . . .

MAN Then you should. Go ahead. Rest.

GIRL Thanks.

Without asking, she lays her head in the MAN'*s lap.*

GIRL I like this music . . .

MAN . . . some girl told me about it . . .

GIRL Ha! You're funny.

MAN Not very.

GIRL Sometimes . . . (*Beat.*) You sure you don't want me to blow you or anything?

MAN Please don't say that stuff.

GIRL Most guys would, just so you know . . . even if I was their niece and they ended up in this same situation? I'm telling you the truth: *lots* of guys would let me do it. (*Smiles.*) And I've been told that I give lovely head. Seriously. That exact word. "Lovely."

MAN Shhhh. Just listen to the . . . (*Checking his watch.*) I'll wake you when it's time.

GIRL Don't forget.

MAN I won't.

GIRL Promise?

MAN Yes. I promise.

GIRL 'Kay.

MAN Goodnight.

GIRL 'Night.

MAN . . . love you.

GIRL . . . mmmmmmm . . .

He sits quietly, careful not to rouse her. One hand moves to touch her but he stops just short. Refraining.

She closes her eyes, starts to drift. She slips her thumb into her mouth.

Without opening her eyes, she says:

GIRL This is ok, right? What I'm doing? Isn't it?

MAN Uh-huh. (*Beat.*) Yes, *Amber*. Everything's just fine . . .

Together they sit and listen to the music. MAN *and* GIRL. *Connected now, if only for the moment.*

Silence. Darkness.

THE GREAT WAR

The Great War had its American premiere at Ensemble Studio Theater in New York City in May 2008. It was directed by Andrew McCarthy.

MAN   Grant Shaud
WOMAN   Laila Robins

NOTE: A slash (/) indicates the point of overlap in interrupted dialogue.

Silence. Darkness.

A living room. A MAN *and a* WOMAN *seated—staring at each other over drinks. An eternity follows (a minute or two).*

MAN   . . . can I just say what I think?

WOMAN   Of course.

MAN   I mean, before we get all . . .

WOMAN   I said "yes."

MAN   No, no, but *honestly* say it and not have to, you know—withstand, like, *gale force* winds in return?

WOMAN   Please.

MAN   What?

WOMAN   Don't start . . .

MAN   *What?*

WOMAN   You *know*. Don't. Start.

MAN   "Don't start?"

WOMAN   That's right. *Don't.*

MAN   Excuse me . . . you don't think it's a little late for that? Hmm?/ I think we're about a *lifetime* past "don't start."

WOMAN   Whatever./ Just . . .

MAN   It's true.

WOMAN   You're so . . . fine. Go ahead.

MAN If you'd said "don't start" to me on that Club Med trip we wouldn't be sitting here right now . . . nine years of pretty-much-Hell behind us.

WOMAN True.

MAN We'd be safe and happy.

WOMAN I know.

MAN I might be seated next to someone I really loved and be making plans for Christmas in *Barbados*, so take it a bit easy with the "don't starts," ok?/ I mean . . .

WOMAN Fine./ No, it's true. I should've gone with a "fuck you, you *boring* little prick" but I decided to give you a chance, so . . .

MAN Ha! Good one.

WOMAN That's what I get for being nice.

MAN Exactly.

WOMAN . . . *and* forgetting my credit card. (*Beat.*) Amazing what I'll endure for a *Mai Tai*.

They pause for a moment—sip at their respective drinks.

MAN Well, at least you won't have to "endure" it any more, right?

WOMAN What's that?

MAN This. *Us*.

WOMAN That's true.

MAN Must be a relief . . . it is to me.

WOMAN Well, good. That's great . . . I'm just really pleased that it's all going so nicely for you. (*Mock sigh.*) That is *terrific*.

MAN Oh, fuck you. Okay?

WOMAN Ha! We're so far past that having any impact—just so you know.

MAN Fine, I'll remember that.

WOMAN Do. (*Beat.*) Save it for the kids—they still get scared when you scream or swear. Use it on them.

MAN You are . . . God! Such a bitch.

WOMAN Thanks.

MAN No, I don't mean anything by it, a value judgment or whatever . . . but, man, you really are. You're a *total* bitch.

WOMAN Asshole.

MAN Uh-huh. (*Beat.*) And for the record? That one doesn't really have much impact, either. Alright? Might as well add it to your list there . . .

WOMAN Yeah . . . (*Smiles.*) Shit, pretty soon we're gonna have to go back to calling each other by our *real* names.

MAN Exactly! (*Laughs.*) That's true.

The MAN *makes a little "toast" with his glass. They drink up.*

MAN . . . so. What're we gonna do?

WOMAN What do you mean?

MAN How does this end—what's the next step?

WOMAN We go on . . . we do what we've been doing and we push on.

MAN Yeah?

WOMAN Yes. To the end. To the end of *us*. Of course. Absolutely./ *God*, yes.

MAN Fine./ Alright, Jesus . . . I was just asking.

WOMAN I mean, *obviously*. (*Beat.*) Sometimes you're such an imbecile./ It really is breathtaking.

MAN Ok, fuck, I know!/ I didn't mean . . . I'm aware we're going to end it, I'm not . . . I meant specifically.

WOMAN Oh.

MAN What're some of the *specifics* that you've been thinking about since . . . you know, since I've been out of the house.

WOMAN Ahhh. I see. Sorry. (*Thinks.*) Well, keep you out, that's one. Keep you out of my house at all costs—that is the first thing. (*Beat.*) Today's an exception, of course . . .

MAN 'Course. (*Beat.*) I like how my being gone for three months can suddenly make this "your" house. Amazing how that happens . . .

WOMAN That's how "abandonment" works, my dear./ Seriously, it would be smart if you sat down with a lawyer at some point. Just for . . .

MAN "Abandonment!"/ That is so fucking *choice* . . . I mean it. That's rich. To say that you're . . . "A-*ban*-don-ment."

WOMAN That's what the nice woman told me. She assures me it'll stick . . .

MAN Oh God, I don't doubt it. I do not *doubt* it for a millisecond. (*Beat.*) I'm sure your lady attorney there is the bee's knees at what she does for you—certainly seems like it from the size of her retainer.

WOMAN Life's a bitch, what can I tell ya?

MAN "Life's a bitch—and then you marry one!" I thought that was the joke.

WOMAN No baby—the joke's on you. Get it?

MAN Cunt.

WOMAN Sorry, but that's on the list, too, so don't overuse it, ok?

MAN You really are . . .

WOMAN Sorry, what? I can't hear you . . .

MAN Jesus Christ. (*Beat.*) How does this happen? Huh? How do we ever get to this place, where you can't even stand the fucking . . . *thought* of a person, you know? Some specific person, let alone be around 'em? HOW?

WOMAN Day by day.

MAN I guess.

WOMAN Day-by-fucking-day. And you work at it, like anything else. You work and work and one day you've done it, dream come true. You despise that person you said you'd love forever. De*test* them. (*Beat.*) It's evolution, baby.

MAN . . . It's bleak, that's what it is.

WOMAN It's life.

MAN No, it's . . . yeah, maybe. Maybe so.

WOMAN It is. We're fickle, us folks.

MAN That's true.

WOMAN We are one fickle bunch.

MAN I suppose so.

WOMAN I *know* so . . . (*Beat.*) Except in first marriages, no offense. I don't know why that is. Maybe because we think we're missing something . . .

MAN . . . I dunno . . .

WOMAN Or going to . . . feel like we're about to miss out on some great romantic secret that everybody but us is in on. So we rush off and do it . . .

MAN Do what?

WOMAN Marry. We jump in and marry the first *schmuck* who asks us—give ourselves away to the very first person who smiles at us or buys us drinks or takes us to bed. (*Beat.*) We are so fucking easy, most of us . . . fickle *and* easy. A deadly combination.

The MAN *nods at this, then considers. Clears his throat.*

MAN . . . I wasn't the first guy who asked you to marry them. I mean, that's not what you said.

WOMAN I know.

MAN So . . .

WOMAN I was referring to you. *You* jumped at the chance when I agreed to marry you.

MAN That's true. (*Smiles.*) Hey, that's funny!

WOMAN What is?

MAN The "schmuck" thing you said—with your scenario there. It's you that made the . . . *you're* the schmuck. Ha!

WOMAN God . . . and don't I know it.

MAN Yeah, so why'd you do it, then? I mean, if I suck *so* much, even back then . . . why would you go and marry me? Hmm? Answer *that* . . .

The MAN *stands and crosses to a bowl of nuts. Takes a few while the* WOMAN *considers what he's just said. He returns.*

WOMAN Safety, I suppose . . . / I think so, anyway.

MAN "Safety?"/ The hell does that mean?

WOMAN You were like . . . my safety school. (*Smiles.*) When you're picking places to go to, as a student? You were my fall-back, my *junior* college. Safe. Cheap./ You were "within walking distance."

MAN That is bullshit . . . / No, that's . . .

WOMAN Is it?

MAN Yeah. You're . . . *yes*.

WOMAN Whatever lets you get to sleep, I guess. (*Beat.*) It's alright, baby, don't worry about it . . . you can't help it that you ended up such a *nothing* of a man . . .

MAN My God, you're . . . no. Uh-uh. Don't say that./ *Shit* like that.

WOMAN What?/ I don't know what you're . . .

MAN *That*. About me. The kids shouldn't hear things like that. All of your negative . . . crap . . .

WOMAN They don't. I fib to them, all the time . . . about you, life, stuff like that. I conjure up stories and make it all o-k. That's my job now, that is what I've become. A professional liar.

MAN I see./ No, I'm . . . I get that . . . what you're *suggesting*, I mean.

WOMAN I doubt it./ You probably don't.

MAN Seriously, I do. You're protecting them from what you consider is . . .

WOMAN The truth. What the truth is. Who you are, what this has become . . .

MAN . . . but it's . . .

WOMAN What?

MAN I mean, you loved me once. Right? Not now, maybe, but back then . . .

WOMAN Really?

MAN *Yes.* I know you did./ Once.

WOMAN You might be right./ It's possible.

MAN Of course you did! You . . . when they were running around in the yard or, or playing board games with them, the dice in our hands and laughing./ At some point during all that . . .

WOMAN Ok./ Maybe. It's—I honestly can't remember now.

MAN Well, I don't care what you say—you did. You loved me and I loved you for awhile there. We were . . . yes.

The WOMAN *can't help but smile at the* MAN*'s earnestness.*

WOMAN Hmmm. (*Beat.*) Somewhere during our nine years of "pretty-much-Hell?" At some point in there?

MAN Yes. During that. (*Beat.*) Listen, I just said that because . . . you know. Because.

WOMAN To hurt me.

MAN . . . yeah. Probably so. (*Beat.*) And . . . I mean . . . I'm just
   talking here, so don't . . . but you would never even consider for
   . . . us . . . you know . . . ?

WOMAN What?

MAN I dunno! Trying again, I guess. Try to just . . . whatever. Again.
   Us.

WOMAN Ummmmmm . . .

The woman considers this for a moment. Laughs. Covers her mouth.

WOMAN No. God, no . . . not ever!/ *Never.*

MAN Ok./ Alright.

WOMAN Not in a million . . . you know. Whatever you want to count
   with. (*Beat.*) Not if we were plopped down on some desert isle
   like . . . if you were that *Robinson Crusoe* guy, I'd still fucking hate
   you./ So . . . no. Uh-uh.

She looks over at the MAN *and starts to say something else but
catches herself. Laughs. Almost to the point of crying.*

MAN Fine./ Okay, I get it! Shit!! I was just trying to . . . forget it.

WOMAN Fine.

MAN I wasn't—it wasn't for me, anyway. (*Beat.*) I was thinking of the
   kids. For *their* sake.

WOMAN Oh.

MAN Yeah.

WOMAN I see . . . for the kids. *Our* kids.

MAN Yes. For them.

WOMAN We could maybe stick it out for them?/ Another dozen years
   or so?

MAN Something like that . . . / Yeah.

WOMAN So that they could have a more . . . I dunno, *stable* environment in which to . . . right?

MAN Along those lines, yes. (*Beat.*) It wasn't a . . . I mean, most studies show that children who've been . . .

WOMAN Honey, no offense but most *studies* don't have to sleep in the same bed with you, alright? Most studies are not gonna have to get down and give you a *blow job*, so that's . . .

MAN Fuck you./ "List" or not . . .

WOMAN I'm just saying . . . / Ha! Good one.

MAN You're such a . . . shit! I mean . . .

The WOMAN *catches herself and doesn't respond. A silence.*

WOMAN *Most* of the governmental studies you see in your *USA Today* are not ever going to have to spend any time at the dinner table staring over at your ineffectual little face and wishing that a piece of fucking *satellite* would drop on the house . . . I mean it, that this chunk of MIR would plummet right down on the dining room as you're picking bits of roast beef out of your teeth with the edge of a business card—so, please, I *beg* you, please spare me any of your snappy "fun facts." (*Waits.*) The kids—whom you probably could not even *name* if they were the final question on *Jeopardy!*—are going to be better off without the kind of death cloud we've had hanging over our marriage the last few years. *Believe* me.

MAN . . . true.

WOMAN Ok?

MAN Yeah. It's . . . maybe you're right.

WOMAN I am. I *know* it. (*Beat.*) No offense.

The MAN *looks over at her—he's the one to laugh out loud this time.*
A short, painful burst.

MAN *Thanks.*

WOMAN My pleasure.

MAN I'm sure . . .

WOMAN Honestly. I don't say any of that with malice, I just—if
we're gonna do this, and we are, then it has to start from a place
of complete and utter honesty.

MAN Right.

WOMAN And the honest truth is: we do not like each other any more.
At all. Not one little bit.

MAN I know, but . . . it's . . .

WOMAN *That* is our reality now, not some "remember when?"
bullshit. No. Our present-day situation is that I'm living alone, I'm
getting divorced and I regret every goddamn *second* that I ever
wasted on this. Every one of them . . . seriously makes me want to
weep and cry out in rage and shame and anger. *That's* where
we're at, right there. *That* is the "us" you speak of.

MAN Geez. (*Beat.*) This is . . . huh. Turning out to be a brutally honest
Tuesday on the Mickey Mouse club, isn't it?

WOMAN It absolutely is. Yes.

MAN Alright then. (*Sighs.*) Ok, so let's make sure that we . . . you
know. Yes. Great. Let's do this.

WOMAN What's that?

MAN You know, whatever. Get down to it.

WOMAN . . . isn't that what we're doing?

MAN Yeah, sure it is, yes, but let's . . . you know. Do the nitty-gritty.

WOMAN . . . meaning . . . ?

MAN You *know.* Let's start dividing up the spoils. And stuff.

The WOMAN *looks over at him and studies his face. Scowls.*

WOMAN *That's* what you wanna talk about?

MAN No, I just . . . I mean . . .

WOMAN That's why you called and said you "had" to see me?

MAN Look, don't make me sound like some *bad* dude here—I just can't talk in that place, when we're sitting in a conference room somewhere./ Thought we could maybe . . . so I suggested . . .

WOMAN Ok./ No, fine. So let's talk about our *stuff*. (*Pointing.*) You want that lamp, or should I . . . ?

MAN Stop! (*Beat.*) We really should do it at some point. This./ Divide stuff up . . .

WOMAN Sure./ We absolutely should.

MAN I mean, seems like the right thing to do . . . the perfect time. While we are being so damn "honest." Right?

WOMAN I'm . . . I agree. (*Beat.*) Why not?

MAN No reason whatsoever. It's about that time.

WOMAN Yes. Let's.

The MAN *gets up, goes to make himself yet another drink.*

MAN Alright. (*He settles back down.*) Ok, so . . . you go first. And don't be all clever and shit, please; don't talk about the *lamps*. I didn't mean all the individual—I don't want to be petty about this.

WOMAN . . . thank God for that . . .

MAN Come on, can we just . . . ? I'm trying to be serious here and get through one conversation about the future without spitting at each other like two, you know, *cobras* or something.

WOMAN Okay. (*Beat.*) I'm pretty sure cobras attack other things, though . . .

The MAN *looks at her, uncertain. He hesitates then speaks:*

MAN . . . no? Do they?

WOMAN Think so./ Uh-huh. They don't waste time trying to kill their own kind.

MAN Really?/ Huh.

WOMAN It was on the TV . . . (*Beat.*) And you really think the two of us can divy up the, like, *silverware* and shit? In our present state?

MAN Ummmmm . . . I honestly don't know, but I'd like to try. If you will. In a general way, I'm saying . . .

WOMAN No, sure, it could be . . . yes. Go-for-it. I'm . . .

The WOMAN *looks off again, starts to stand up but abruptly sits back down. The* MAN *watches her. Shakes his head.*

MAN Alright then . . . that's . . . (*He pulls a sheet of paper out of his pocket.*) I just jotted down a few . . . so let me see . . .

WOMAN Well, well—aren't we prepared?

MAN No, it's no big . . . I did it on the way over here. (*Glances at her.*) I mean, at breakfast. During that.

WOMAN Huh. I see. (*Beat.*) So?

The MAN *shifts around a bit, trying to assert some sort of authority. To make it all sound proper. He sits down again.*

MAN So, look, I'll be honest here . . .

WOMAN . . . that should be *interesting* . . .

MAN Jesus, fuck, do you have to? Hmm?! After, like, every word or phrase, do you absolutely have to make a face or say something or, or, you know, throw your little *hex* on it? I'm curious, I seriously am . . . are you *compelled* to do that or what?

WOMAN No. Obviously no. (*Beat.*) It's just funny sometimes./ It amuses me.

MAN I see./ Great.

WOMAN And it keeps me from crying my eyes out over this every single moment. Over how we've thrown our lives out the window —and yes, I'm including you here, too—both of us have just tossed away our youth and beauty on a shitty little life together that amounted to exactly zero. *Less* than that, maybe. Less than zero and I'm sorry but that makes me sad so I'll sometimes joke. Or try to hurt you. Or whatever. (*Beat.*) That's the way I am. Forgive me.

MAN No, I get that. I do. I mean . . . when you put it that way.

WOMAN Good.

MAN 'Cause I pretty much hate you, too! (*Beat.*) In my own "ineffectual" way, of course.

WOMAN Touché, baby. Touché.

The MAN *drains his drink and sets the glass aside. The* WOMAN *waits.*

WOMAN . . . how about reading me your list there? Should be amusing.

MAN It's not meant to be . . . I think this stuff's important. Every bit of it. As meaningful as—I don't know what I'm saying. Forget it. (*Folds over the paper.*) We can just figure this out with your attorney, I guess . . .

WOMAN No, no, come on . . . I was just messing around. You're right about it. (*Beat.*) See? For once I'm being nice to you—this might be the simplest, least combative scenario for us . . . just talking.

MAN Okay. (*Beat.*) Alright then. Fine.

WOMAN So? Go ahead.

MAN Ummmm . . . (*Reopens paper.*) I sort've split things into . . . you know, like, categories. You understand what I'm saying.

WOMAN Sure. I mean, I know the *word*. It's "categories." I get it.

The MAN *stands to read, giving it a bit of gravitas.*

MAN Good . . . (*Beat.*) Should we start with the . . . doesn't feel right to discuss our boat when we . . . or the timeshare when we have—those're just things, that's all. Items. *Junk.* So if you want all the paintings and mirrors or the, the . . . just say so. Do. But that's not why I'm being . . . all . . .

WOMAN Thank you. *So* generous.

MAN No, come on, you know what I'm saying here—let's get down to what's important. The substance. All the real . . . the stuff we never get to talk about.

WOMAN What?

MAN Not what . . . who.

WOMAN "Who?" (*Beat.*) Ok, now I'm lost.

MAN Jesus, come on. The *kids*. How about them in all this? I think it's time for us to . . .

WOMAN Keep 'em.

MAN Excuse me?

The WOMAN *says nothing more and the* MAN *doesn't know what to do now; he sits down, folding the paper up again as he does.*

WOMAN Keep-them. I don't want them or anything to do with 'em. Really.

MAN Come on, be serious.

WOMAN I am.

MAN Alright, if you're not gonna treat this as a . . .

WOMAN I *am* treating it with complete and utter seriousness, sweetheart: You-may-have-the-children.

MAN I'm . . . what? That's not what we've been—you've let this drag on for *months* saying that you're . . . that we had to come to some sort of . . .

WOMAN Yes? Tell me . . .

MAN I don't know! That you were, like, after money for them and how many days of school holiday that I can see . . . you know what I'm saying! You have pitched a *battle* in defense of them.

WOMAN No, I haven't; you misunderstand me again./ Yes. Like always.

MAN Oh, *really*?/ No, I haven't . . .

WOMAN You've looked at the *facts* and not been at all able to *understand* 'em.

MAN Then why don't you explain it to me then. Ok? Like you would a 4th grader and I'll sit here and listen and try to keep up. (*Beat.*) Go on.

She is about to respond but catches herself. Stops. She regroups and speaks slowly. Clearly.

WOMAN Fine. I didn't do it for them, any of it, the fighting or nagging or long-winded letters in the official-looking envelopes. No. I did not./ I did it *against* you.

MAN So then . . . / *What*?

WOMAN I did it for spite and revenge. To squander your money and your time. To bother you.

MAN Oh.

WOMAN That's why.

MAN I see. Not because . . .

WOMAN No. Not because I should've or was supposed to. Not as a mother or as some angel of mercy. And certainly not *for* them . . .

MAN God. I mean, that's . . . *shit*.

WOMAN I've never really liked them. You know? I mean, when it comes right down to it . . . I get none of those gooey-lovely things when I look at my children. *Feelings*. All I see is you. I see you in them and that is enough to make me sick, makes me want to gouge out their eyes and bruise their lips, tear them off their little faces—to erase all traces of you in them. *That's* what I see each morning as I get them ready for school. (*Beat.*) So that's fine, really. It's silly for me to go on this way, to spend so much energy on such negativity—have them if you want to. I don't give a shit any more.

MAN . . . ummm . . .

WOMAN I'm serious. I'm through with the trench warfare here, the attrition and all that. Let's just let it be over; you want them so damn badly you're welcome to 'em. The *kiddies*.

MAN But that's not . . . you're . . .

WOMAN One of each. It'll be nice for you. Like new bookends or something. You get that and I get to walk away.

MAN Yeah, but you can't just . . . *honey* . . .

WOMAN Of course I can. Of *course*. That's what adults do—we have to make the big, hard choices. We rarely do it, we follow the path and play by the rules, do the same shit and blunder through the exact goddamn mistakes as our parents did . . . but we are, in fact, *allowed*. If we want to, if we are bold enough to . . . we can do anything we want. *Any*. Thing. And our children, by virtue of being that, "children," must follow along.

MAN Oh. (*Beat.*) Wow, God, that's so . . .

WOMAN Look, it was you who spoke so highly—and at *such* great
length—about having a family. How important and terrific it would
be./ Not me.

MAN Yeah, but . . . / Honey, listen . . .

WOMAN It was just another heap in a huge pile of shit you were
selling. The American Dream. How lovely. How so so perfect and
happy we would be . . . (*Beat.*) In case you haven't noticed:
We're not.

MAN Yeah, no, I get that. Loud and clear. Yes.

WOMAN Then my work here is done. (*Stands.*) Keep them. Help 'em
with their homework and make 'em their meals. Get *nothing* in
return. Knock yourself out. I'm sick of it—I didn't know it was a
fucking life sentence when I signed on, you know? You and them
and it just . . . it never ends! It is endless. No matter what I do,
what else happens in life . . . every day finishes with me wiping
somebody's ass for them and I have had enough.

The WOMAN *moves to go but the* MAN *stands—not blocking her way
but causing her to stop. Listen.*

MAN No, no, no, no . . . this is not what I, you know . . . had in
mind when I first . . . wait!

WOMAN Have-them. Go on. They're not that *special*, trust me. You'll
find that out within a week . . .

MAN . . . Jesus . . .

WOMAN *Please*. Come on, no one's watching, they're not keeping
score here—be real about this. You were never at home, what
would you know about it? How could you possibly have a sense
of who or what they are . . . how they turned out?

MAN Don't say that . . . I mean, Jesus, do not be *hateful* for the
sheer sake of it. I know that they're . . . that my children are . . .
are . . .

A silence gradually settles in. The MAN *stops talking.*

WOMAN Exactly. You don't know shit.

MAN . . . no, I suppose I . . . no.

WOMAN These are not *chemists* we're talking about here, international prizewinners, future finders of *vaccines* to save the planet.
No. We didn't bring forth any geniuses, you and I . . . that is both
our blessing and our curse. They are just normal and average,
straight-up kids who will grow sullen and pensive because of what
we are doing to them, who will learn to smile and say that everything is alright, to cry at night when others are sleeping, and learn
to plot and plan and divide us like wolves splitting up the calves
from the herd. They're frighteningly normal, these kids of ours—
casualties of war, the walking wounded who will excel at nothing
but revenge toward you and me. That is who they are. (*Smiling
sadly.*) They are not part of some great generation coming back
from the greatest of wars, leaving the battlefields of Verdun and
the Somme and heading back toward the waiting arms of those
Jazz-Aged, bob-haired beauties, struck dumb by horror and
carnage and a world out of balance. Sipping champagne while
dancing off into the night, or down to Spain to watch a noonday
bullfight in some small country town in the vain hope that this
new pleasure might somehow, in *some* way ease their pain . . .
(*Beat.*) Those are not our children, my dearest. Oh no. We have
two "C" students who will probably work in *insurance* somewhere
and, if family genetics have anything to say . . .

MAN   . . . don't, please . . .

WOMAN   . . . they will die, quite probably, of heart disease in their
mid to late 60s. *That* is the legacy we have left behind. Yours
and mine.

MAN   No. (*Beat.*) No, no, no!

WOMAN   No?

MAN   *No* . . . that's not . . . you're wrong.

WOMAN   And how's that?

MAN   NO. That is *not* who my children are or have become./ You
don't know all there is to . . . you couldn't.

WOMAN   Really?/ Is that right?

MAN   And you've got the facts all . . . the "Great War," "the Greatest
Generation" . . . that's not them, or even us. It was our parents
who . . . the ones who fought in World War Two. *That* was the
"great" war, not the first one. In Europe at the turn of the . . . no.
That was "The war to end all wars." And it was a dumb name,
anyway, because, well . . . I mean, obviously. People still go off
and kill each other so that's a bust, far as I'm concerned. It didn't
really end anything. (*Beat.*) So . . . I mean, is that right or have I got
those all twisted around?

WOMAN   Doesn't matter. You know what I'm saying . . . I was simply . . .

MAN   Yeah, I do. *Yes.* Some hateful shit. About our boys, our sweet
little . . .

WOMAN   Please. Stop.

MAN   No, I'm serious here . . .

WOMAN   I have to play this game with my lawyer-lady and the
judge and each time I visit their classrooms, all the times that
I do it. *Me.* Okay? So today is—just as you pointed out—
"honest day" here at Mickey's place. The kids don't mean
shit to me. Nothing . . . (*Beat.*) There was a time, years ago,

a glimmer of hope when they were born, each a falling star into our lives that suggested maybe . . . just maybe . . . we were somehow going to make it as a couple. But not any more. Now they're nothing but bargaining chips, pawns that you and I and our very expensive associates love to keep pushing across the board at each other. But as *people*? People that I'd pick out as friends or family or even neighbors? They're third-stringers at best. At *best*.

MAN . . . Good God . . .

WOMAN The truth, as always, burns like a motherfucker, and the *truth*, ugly as it may seem, is . . . our kids are nothing to write home about. Ever. Even if you were half-way through an email . . . (*Beat.*) Baby, I'm giving you my absolutely honest opinion here: you want 'em, you go ahead and have 'em. I'll even throw in the Lexus./ I will . . .

MAN What?/ Are you serious?

WOMAN Completely. It's only got twelve thousand miles on it . . .

MAN I can't believe this! I mean . . .

WOMAN Think about it. No rush.

MAN How can you even . . . ?!

WOMAN Easy . . . (*Beat.*) I can't look at them without seeing their father, a tiny piece in anything they do or say or wish . . . I told you this before . . . and that makes me want to drown them in the tub, makes me wish that I could leave them in the mall or choke 'em in their sleep—do what*ever* I need to do to wipe the last of *you* off their little brows . . . (*Beat.*) That person, someone who feels like that, really shouldn't be making their meals, now, should they?

MAN . . . no. No, probably not. But . . . / This . . . I mean, this is . . . *shit* . . .

WOMAN *What*?/ You don't really wanna split 'em up, do you?

MAN No! God, no. They're young . . . they should be together. With

their . . .

WOMAN Exactly. Together.

MAN But this is—and you don't want 'em again because why?

'Cause they're not, like, these two amazing—they are eight and

five, by the way—because they're not off-the-charts at school yet

or, or, like, musical *prodigies*? Huh? I mean, that's just not . . .

aww, fuck! Fuck, fuck, FUCK!!

WOMAN Exactly. Which started all this, in the first place . . .

They look at each other. Both burst out laughing. Loudly.

MAN You are funny, I'll give you that.

WOMAN Thanks.

MAN That was always nice.

WOMAN Thank you. You're sweet. (*Beat.*) So come on, let's do

this . . .

MAN What?

WOMAN You know. Get down to it—split up the loot. (*Beat.*) I have

a facial at three.

MAN And I'm seeing Rex over at the club for . . . (*Trails off.*) God,

listen to us!

WOMAN Hmm?

MAN No, I just . . . it's like the *Wannsee Conference* or something.

Us here.

WOMAN Honey, I never really did take an interest in your work,

so . . .

MAN No, the Wannsee . . . forget it. (*Beat.*) So, what do we do?/

Yes?

WOMAN Well . . . / It's obvious how I feel, what I want . . . or at least would prefer.

MAN . . . alright . . .

WOMAN But you haven't said a word, I mean not really, about what you want—

MAN Yes, I have . . . / I've . . .

WOMAN No, uh-uh, not really./ What you're *programmed* to feel, but not what-you-want./ Yes, of course it does! Tell me. Go on.

MAN It doesn't matter./ But this isn't how . . . I worry about coming off . . .

WOMAN *Don't*. Just say it. Be free and be honest and say what you're actually thinking . . . / Go ahead.

MAN But . . . / This isn't how a grown . . . being selfish or, or *hating*, like how you . . . I'm a, I am an *adult* . . .

The MAN *catches himself and stops for a moment. Considers. He turns to the* WOMAN, *a bit wide-eyed. Speaks bluntly.*

MAN . . . oh my god. (*Beat.*) I don't like children! I don't. Not just ours but any. All. Everywhere. That's just . . . I mean, it's not that I'm, I wasn't loved or, or . . . just the opposite probably, now that I think about it . . . (*He shudders.*) I believe I might've even been loved *too* much. Yes. I don't really wanna go there right now, though. (*Shakes his head.*) I'm not sure I understand it or why . . . I wanted to, felt like I was *supposed* to so I talked it up, was all gung-ho to you about the prospect . . . but in the end, I don't like 'em. Sorry. Didn't wanna have them, probably should've said something, *years* ago, but it felt rude at the time and so, you know, you just go with the flow . . . and now here we are, two little *tots* caught in the midst of our crap and I don't wanna hurt them, not outright, anyway, but no way do I have the room in my new place and it's just . . . their schools are way over in . . . / And so that's a whole . . . Jesus . . . oh God.

WOMAN See?/ It's ok! It's human to be a little selfish . . . *but* there's the world to contend with./ What people think and do and feel about us . . .

MAN True./ Right.

WOMAN So what I propose is this: joint custody.

MAN . . . you're kidding, right?

WOMAN Not at all./ Just listen.

MAN But . . . / Alright.

WOMAN We get out our calendars, mark off the days that make the most sense for ourselves and check that with the other person's list and presto! We've come to a begrudging detente. Our friends and neighbors see us as profoundly human, making sacrifices for the wee ones and life goes on. We have played the game. We've won the war. Somehow, through lies and subterfuge and, and great *personal* cost—we have come out of this mess looking like actual human beings.

MAN So . . . you mean . . . we do the same old shit that anybody else would do in this position?

WOMAN Exactly! We *pretend*.

MAN Oh. (*It finally clicks.*) Ohhhhh! So, we'll *act* like we care . . . / As if we are sweet and good and filled with the milk of . . . human kindness . . .

WOMAN Yes!/ Exactly. That is exactly what we'll do.

MAN Huh. Ok. (*Beat.*) Now *that* makes sense.

The MAN *slips his hand across the great divide of the couch and touches the* WOMAN*'s hand. Meeting her gaze.*

MAN But seriously, though . . . what *are* we going to do about the boat?

WOMAN You can keep the boat.

MAN *Really?*

WOMAN Yes, keep it . . . but I want the dog. I *love* the dog.

MAN I keep the boat if you get the dog? (*Beat.*) Yes?

WOMAN Yes.

MAN Ok.

WOMAN Ok.

MAN Fine.

WOMAN Fine.

MAN Good. (*Beat.*) Alright then. You've got yourself a deal . . .

They continue to touch. Staring out at the audience. Smiling.

Silence. Darkness.

IN THE BEGINNING

In the Beginning had its American premiere at Theater Row in New York City in January 2013 (as part of a series of short plays collectively titled *Theatre Uncut*.) It was directed by Emily Reutlinger.

PARENT   Victor Slezak
CHILD   Gia Crovatin

Silence. Darkness.

Two people standing in a room. PARENT *and his only* CHILD.

They stand in silence for a beat, staring at each other.

*If this is done elsewhere (school cafeteria, park, living room, etc.),
then just make-believe—that's what theater is supposed to be about,
after all.*

PARENT . . . I don't think so.

CHILD You don't *think* so?

PARENT That's what I said.

CHILD So that's "no" then, right?

PARENT Is it?

CHILD *Isn't* it?

PARENT Pretty much. Yes.

CHILD I see.

PARENT Good.

CHILD I mean, you love to say "we'll see" or "I don't know."
"*Maybe.*" You love all those phrases but what you really mean is
"no." You're saying "no" to me. Correct?

PARENT Yes, I am . . . if you wanna put it that way, then yes, I'm
saying *no*. Absolutely not. I'm *finally* drawing the line. Right here.

CHILD You're refusing to help me . . . is that it?

PARENT No, that's not . . . no. I "help" you *all* the time, your *whole* life I've *helped* you . . .

CHILD That's not what I mean.

PARENT I know you don't. You never do, you don't state the facts when you're screaming at me, telling me what an *asshole* I am . . .

CHILD I don't do that.

PARENT No? *Really*?

CHILD I mean, yes, we've . . . we fight sometimes, argue about things—*politics* or, or, or, other stuff, *religion*—but I don't just go around calling you names. No, I don't.

PARENT You've never called me an "asshole?" Not to my *face*? In *public*?

CHILD I mean . . .

PARENT Because I feel like I can recall a time or two . . . an instance or three when you've done that. That very word.

CHILD But, that's . . . not . . .

PARENT Belittled me. Humiliated me. In front of your friends or your fellow . . . rioters. Occupiers.

CHILD *One* time! If you're talking about when I was down there in the park and . . . you . . . you tried to get me to come . . . home . . .

PARENT . . . when *I* brought you food . . . carried this overflowing *box* of sandwiches and drinks down to you . . . that's what I did.

CHILD Mom made you do that! *Mom* did!

PARENT Yes, maybe so, but *I* carried it! I did it for you . . . brought them to you and all the other . . . *whatevers* . . . they are! *I* did that!

CHILD Ok, fine . . . thank you . . .

PARENT I don't want that, I'm not asking for any thanks for *school* or your *rent* or the airline ticket to *Iceland* so you could be on the news . . . be seen 'round the world tossing a *firebomb* at that hotel

. . . I do not need your thanks for that. *No. (Beat.)* All I'm saying is I can't help you this time. Not any longer . . . *every*body has a tipping point and I've hit mine. This is *it*.

CHILD But people . . . Dad, people still need help! *Our* help. To be heard . . . to have a chance. *(Beat.)* Look, I'm not asking you to sign on here or to even understand completely. All I want is for you to just *respect* my decision to do this . . . to give of myself and to . . . you know . . . *give*.

PARENT Give *what*? You never speak in specifics!

CHILD That's not true. You *don't* listen!

PARENT Ok, fine . . . this is me doing just that. I am shutting up and listening, so tell me. Go ahead. What-do-you-stand-for?

CHILD We're not . . . it isn't just *one* thing! It's *lots* of things. The homeless and, and . . . what the banks have done . . . look at what students are doing right now! Going back to grad school, *deeper* into debt because there aren't any jobs out there, nothing! *(Beat.)* And I believe in these people, in helping give voice to *all* of them and in *any* way that I can. *That* is what I wanna do . . . *that's* what I wanna be a part of.

PARENT Then fine, go. Do it. Use the last bit of your savings and go to New York and *shit* in the park for days upon days so that I and everybody who *does* work for a living can be *scolded* by you and your kind . . . so we *comprehend* that we've all done a very bad thing here. I am not stopping you . . .

CHILD I know you're not, that's not what I'm . . . *(Beat.)* I don't have enough in my account. I need some money. Please.

PARENT You need me to—wait, lemme just get this straight, so I understand the—you'd like *me* to pay for your trip? Buy you *another* seat on a . . . plane or a train or a bus so you can go sleep in a tent and show the world what a shitty job it's done taking care of all the other people who live in tents . . . not just you college kids who do it for a couple weeks because you *care* so much . . . because you *love* this planet and all its peoples so so much . . . but the ones who *actually* don't even have tents, who live in *boxes* or *crates* because that's all they've got? You want me to help you with that? Find some way to get you there safely with a little cash in your pocket . . . is that what you're saying? (*Beat.*) Please, *enlighten* me.

CHILD Look, it could be a loan, or . . . you know from my trust. (*Beat.*) I won't ask again!

PARENT Oh, I know you won't.

CHILD What are you saying?

PARENT I am *saying* you won't ever ask me this again because I can't hear you any more.

CHILD . . . what're you . . . what does that mean?

PARENT It means I am looking forward . . . I have seen the future and it's not you. I had *such* hopes and dreams for you but it is not you or anyone like you. (*Beat.*) Folks like you mean well but in the end, they don't do shit. Nothing. They sit on the grass and smoke a little pot and I don't wanna be a part of that. Buy into that.

CHILD You don't have to *buy* into anything! It is happening right now . . . the world's . . . things are changing right in front of us and I want to be there, to help out when and where I can! I am a part of something that is bigger than just you and me—it's about jobs and corporate responsibility!! I'm not the *problem*, I'm the *solution*! *I* am the future!! *Me*, and people like me!!

PARENT Sorry, but if you're the future then I'm gonna put a gun to my head after dinner and blow my fucking brains out . . .

CHILD I wish you would! I really do!

PARENT I know you do! I KNOW THAT YOU DO! So you can get your inheritance . . . so you'll have the *cash* to keep running around and doing stupid *shit* like you're about to go off and do right now! That's what you always do, you run off and do any shit you want, instead of sticking with something the way I did . . . (*Waits.*) I stayed at a job I didn't like all these years, with a woman I didn't love all these years, in a neighborhood I couldn't afford all these years! For you. For the *hope* that was you.

CHILD . . . what am I supposed to say to that?

PARENT Nothing. It's just the truth. Not a lot you can say about the truth: it just *is*.

CHILD Listen . . . I wasn't even supposed to come home this weekend! I came home for your *birthday*, that was me doing something for you and now you're . . . you won't even give me a ride back into town . . . or, or . . .

The MAN *wheels around, getting up into his* CHILD*'s face.*

PARENT Walk.

CHILD What?

PARENT Walk back . . . if you wanna be there *so* bad that you can't even wait for your friends to pick you up . . . then walk.

CHILD To New York? Walk from *Boston* down to New York City?!

PARENT I mean, if it means that much to you . . .

CHILD That's just ridiculous. I mean . . . come *on*!

PARENT Why?

CHILD Because it would take *days*, that's why!! Because it's *far*!!

PARENT As far as the Pacific?

CHILD I'm . . . I don't even know what you're . . .

PARENT Is it as far as the Pacific Ocean?

The CHILD *stops, thinking for a moment before speaking—finally gives in with a defiant shrug and a sigh.*

CHILD No, it's not as far as that. Satisfied?

PARENT I just mean . . . in the beginning, the first people who wanted to see an ocean or the Arctic . . . Africa, even . . . those first men and women would walk for miles and miles and *miles*. Hundreds or thousands of miles to explore them. Those sights.

CHILD That's—they had horses, too! And *wagons*! Ever heard of "wagon trains?"

PARENT Some of them did. Yes. But not all. Many of the pioneers or settlers in this land or other countries, too . . . if they wanted a thing badly enough then they built it or walked to it or dug it up out of the ground with their own bare hands. That's what people do when they really believe in something or desire it badly enough. They *go* out and *get* it. (*Beat.*) There's the front door . . . New York is due South. Go for it.

CHILD You're *crazy*!

PARENT You're *lazy*!

CHILD No, I'm not! I'm *not*!!

PARENT So prove it . . . get going. I'd take your jacket with you. Gonna be cold tonight.

CHILD I'm not *walking* to New York!

PARENT Then you should go up to your nice room and crawl into your soft bed and forget about the whole thing . . . the choice is yours. The clock is ticking. The time is *now*.

The CHILD *stomps one foot a few times—now tired of being nice.*

CHILD You're . . . God, you're *such* an asshole!!

PARENT I knew we'd get back around to that if I waited long enough . . .

CHILD I hate you! I hate you!! I *hate* you!!!

PARENT And that's really what this is about, isn't it?

CHILD What?

PARENT This "movement" of yours . . . it's a bunch of kiddies who despise their mommies and daddies and so they're taking it out on the whole goddamn planet!

CHILD I'm not doing this for *me*, ok?! This is important! This is *our* future!!

PARENT Says who?!

CHILD *I* DO! THE PEOPLE I ADMIRE DO!!

PARENT Then go paint a banner and start walking! *Do* something if you love 'em so much!!

CHILD I will!

PARENT No you won't! You're a child and you're weak and the weak never win! Not ever!!

CHILD You're wrong . . .

PARENT Keep watching. Stayed tuned, you little fucker.

CHILD If we fail someone else will rise up . . .

PARENT And they'll be crushed back down, just like the ones who came before them . . .

CHILD We are revolutionaries!

PARENT You're freeloaders and parasites—embrace it and I might even respect you.

CHILD I don't *want* your respect!

PARENT Perfect, because you don't have it!

CHILD I've *never* had it! You've *never* liked me! Never, never, NEVER!!

PARENT Ha! See? Told you so.

CHILD What?

PARENT That's the real problem here. It's not at all about Wall Street
. . . it's about "daddy didn't *hold* me enough when I was a baby."

CHILD Are you *kidding* me?! Do you *really* think it's as simple as
that?! *Everything* that we're doing out there?!

PARENT Overall? Yeah, I think so.

CHILD Then you're a fool. You're an old fool whose time has come like
all the other old fools before him . . . we have a mission and a message and I am a part of that. I want to be there to hear those words
and to see great things happen. I wasn't put on this earth to just
keep . . . take, take, taking!! I wanna give back!! We *have* to give
back at some point or it was all for nothing, this crappy little thing
we call *life* was about nothing . . . this is *my* time. This is *my* calling.
I believe that I am making a difference and if I have to burn down
an *embassy* or, or get dragged off to jail a couple times to prove
that point, to show the world that we can't sit by and watch as the
strong *batter* the weak into the dust, I will do that! I will do what
I have to and yes . . . if you make me crawl back to New York on
my hands and knees then I will, I *will*! To be a part of something
great and true and pure . . . and you should support that, support *me*
in that!!! Not because you *agree* with me but because you *believe*
in me!! Believe that *I* believe in it!! (*Going to her knees.*) Please! I beg
you! I am *begging* you here! Please!! (*Beat.*) *Daddy*?

The CHILD *looks up to see how this has landed. The* PARENT *has still
not reacted. The* CHILD *gets up, frustrated.*

CHILD Ahhhhhhhh! If mom were here she'd help me 'cause she
loves me! You hear that? LOVES ME!!

PARENT *I* love you! I love the fucking shit outta you!!

The PARENT *finally relents. Reaches into his pocket and produces a set of keys. Some cash.*

PARENT OH, ALRIGHT! God . . . I'm *such* a pushover! (*Beat.*) Take the Mercedes but do not park on the street. Do you hear me? DO NOT.

CHILD I won't. I promise.

PARENT Here's enough cash for a couple days but I expect you back on the weekend. (*Beat.*) Your mother has your cousins coming over and she wants you to be here, so do *not* let me down. Alright?

CHILD I'll be back Friday night. I *promise*.

PARENT Alright, then. Go. Good luck. Don't get arrested . . .

CHILD I'll do my best . . . but the cops are . . . you know how they are! They *provoke* us!!

PARENT Just listen to me and don't speak: DO NOT GET ARRESTED! I don't wanna drive down to get you out of jail so just . . . do what you do, yell and burn the flag or whatever . . .

CHILD . . . I've never done that! That was not me! That was Tommy, my roommate! *He* did that!

PARENT Fine, fine, just . . . do your thing and try not to kill anybody . . .

CHILD I won't, I promise! (*Beat.*) Thanks, Dad . . .

The CHILD *hugs the* PARENT. *The* PARENT *finally hugs back.*

PARENT Just go . . . I'm sure they need help digging a *latrine* or something . . . passing out *free* condoms!

CHILD Ok, I will.

PARENT Alright. Have fun.

CHILD I'll try . . . (*Smiling.*) You know what, Dad? You're not as bad as you think you are.

PARENT Yeah, yeah, yeah . . .

CHILD I mean, don't get me wrong: you're an asshole . . . but you're a good-hearted asshole.

PARENT Thank you . . . that means a lot. *Sweetie*. (*Beat.*) Shit. Why can't you just go to *rehab*, like *normal* kids do?

Another hug. The CHILD *leaves. The* PARENT *remains behind.*

The PARENT *shakes his head while pulling a cell phone out of a jacket pocket. He pushes a few numbers.*

PARENT . . . yes, hello? Is this the State Patrol? Fine. (*Beat.*) I'd like to report a stolen vehicle. (*Beat.*) Yes, I can hold . . .

Blackout.

THE WAGER

The Wager is a stage adaptation of the short film *Double or Nothing*. The film had its American premiere at the Tribeca International Film Festival in New York City in April 2012. It was directed by Nathaniel Krause.

GUY	Adam Brody
GAL	Louisa Krause
HOMELESS DUDE	Keith David

Silence. Darkness.

A city street. Quiet now as it's getting late (or early, depending on how young you are). A COUPLE—*dressed for a night out—comes out the side exit of a club.*

Nearby is a HOMELESS DUDE, *sitting on the ground with the whole array of personal effects displayed: a dirty piece of cardboard and a ratty sleeping bag, a cart piled high with bags and shit, etc. He's pretty much minding his own business. For now.*

GUY . . . no, no, no, come on, seriously. Can we just go now? *Please*?

GAL *Baby* . . .

GUY Honestly, it's . . . (*Checks watch.*) Sweetie, it's 1:45. In the morning.

GAL I know.

GUY Yeah, well, you may *know* it but I'm *aware* of it, ok? And you know why?

GAL No. Why?

GUY . . . because I gotta work tomorrow! I mean today. I'm have to be at work in, like . . . six hours. (*Kisses her cheek.*) *Six*.

GAL Me too! (*Beat.*) Well, class. I have class tomorrow. Or today. Or . . . whatever!

GUY Uh-huh. At *three*. In the *afternoon*. And it's an *art* class, by the way!

GAL So?

GUY So . . . that's painting. Or pottery or . . . that sorta deal. It's basically *crafts*. Like what kids do . . .

GAL It's for my *Masters*.

GUY Great. *Cool*. Meanwhile, I'm actually going to be *lifting* and *sweating* and shit . . . thus the name "work."

GAL Uh-uh! You're in "sales."

GUY Hey! Hey! We *move* things—signs and, and those big . . . *standees*. All kinds of crap! I'm a very physical guy at work and so . . . yeah. I'm in need of rest.

GAL Fine.

GUY No, not "fine" and you get all quiet now. I came out with you, a *week*night—I'm the guy who does, like, 60 or 70% of all the stuff you wanna do . . . *karaoke* or that one time I went *bowling* even, so just please. *Please*. Do this one thing for me.

GAL Okay. I'm not arguing. I thought we were having fun, but hey . . .

GUY *You* were! You and your girlfriends from the *sketching* class were having a great time but not me, and not half the guys who came with them. Alright? (*Beat.*) You need to glance around once in a while . . . see how everybody else is feeling.

GAL What are you saying? Are you saying I'm selfish now? (*Beat.*) Are you?

GUY . . . no . . . *sweetie* . . . I'm not saying that! I am saying that you're very . . . "focused."

GAL Sounds like you're calling me "selfish."

GUY I don't care what it sounds like . . .

The HOMELESS DUDE *has worked his way over to them by this point.*
He taps the GUY *on the shoulder.*

HOMELESS DUDE . . . hey man, what's up?

The GUY *stops, turns. Bemused by this man.*

GUY Nothing's up, dude. I'm having a private conversation with my
girlfriend. Why?

HOMELESS DUDE That's cool . . .

GUY Yeah, thanks for the *endorsement* there.

HOMELESS DUDE She's pretty. (*Beat.*) Anyways, bro . . .

GAL Honey, let's go. Come on.

Silence. The GAL *wants to go and tugs on the arm of her boyfriend.*
He, however, is staring at the HOMELESS DUDE.

GUY No, hold it. He stopped us, let's see what he wants . . .
(*To* HOMELESS DUDE.) So?

HOMELESS DUDE Hungry, bro, that's all. Can you help a brother out
tonight? It's cold being out here on the street . . .

GUY I'm an only child, so first things first: we're not *brothers*, ya got
that? "Bro?"

HOMELESS DUDE It's cool, that's cool. Okay.

GAL Clark . . .

HOMELESS DUDE Just wanted a little . . . you know . . . anything you
can spare. Know what I mean?

GUY No, what? You people always want *some*thing so it's impossible
to keep up. You want food or money, or, or, *what*? The keys to my
apartment . . . ?

HOMELESS DUDE   *What*? You're talking crazy now . . . what?

The GUY *just stares at the* HOMELESS DUDE. *Watching him.*

GUY   What-do-you-want? Tell me. (*Beat.*) Now.

HOMELESS DUDE   Some *bread*, man! You know that . . .

GUY   You're not, like, a *hippy*, ok? Wrong era, so just stop with the bullshit talk . . . I'm asking you, pretty directly here, what is it you want from us? Hmmm?

HOMELESS DUDE   *Mon-ey*! Come on, man . . . just some change.

GUY   Oh, "just" some change—because we *must* have cash, we're young and white and all that shit, so we *must* be rich.

GAL   Clark, please. I'm cold.

GUY   Sorry. (*To* HOMELESS DUDE.) My girlfriend's cold so I can't really get into it with you right now, like I was gonna, but hey, it's your lucky night . . . I'm gonna teach you the value of money—or in your case, *foodstamps*—which your folks apparently never did . . . probably due to an extended stay in prison and/or a halfway house.

The GUY *reaches into a pocket and produces a dollar bill.*
He holds it in his hand and points to it, using his head to gesture.

GAL   Baby, stop . . . what're you doing?

GUY   I'm giving this dude a job.

GAL   What?

GUY   I'm *offering* this *gentleman* the chance to earn a living wage . . . (*Smiling.*) And learn a little about "Capitalism," too, while he's at it.

GAL   Yeah, while I'm standing here freezing.

GUY   Gimme a minute! (*To* HOMELESS DUDE.) Hey, *Denzel*, come over here a sec'!

The HOMELESS DUDE *keeps staring at the cash. Expectant.*

HOMELESS DUDE Wha's up, man?

GUY *You.* You're up. Step over here and earn your keep or shut the
fuck up . . .

GAL Clark!

GUY What?! Sorry, I'm not swearing *at* him . . . it's just my—doesn't
matter. Just lemme finish. Please. (*He rolls the single into a tiny
ball.*) Ok, dude, you're on.

HOMELESS DUDE What'chu mean?

GUY Here. My two hands. I've got money in there. One dollar . . .
that's at *least* a chicken leg at KFC . . . maybe even a slice of
watermelon. You want it?

The HOMELESS DUDE *looks at the* GUY, *unsure at first what to say. Finally
he blurts out:*

HOMELESS DUDE Hell yeah!

GUY Good, then you gotta *earn* it. Ok? Easy.

HOMELESS DUDE Whatever, man, just gimme it . . .

GUY Not so fast! Hold on there and don't go touching me, either.
You're dirty.

GAL Clark, don't! My God . . . why're you . . . ?

GUY What?! Just stop, please? Okay? It's not *racist*, it's a fact.
Look at him—I'd say it to anybody. It's not a *black*-thing . . . it's
a *soap*-thing. The man is filthy!

HOMELESS DUDE It's not me, bro, it's all the cars and *smoke* and
shit—I'm clean on the inside.

GUY Yeah, what'd I tell you about the "bro" thing, alright? Don't do it
again. I'm serious. (*Beat.*) We've got a . . . massive material divide
between us and I'd like you to respect that. 'Kay? (*Beat.*) O-KAY?

HOMELESS DUDE Fine, bro, fine—sorry, man. I'm sorry. I respect you. I do.

GUY Idiot. (*Looks at the* GAL) Or can't I say that, either? Is *that* wrong now, too?

The GAL *just shrugs her shoulders and shifts her weight from one high-heeled shoe to the other.*

The GUY turns back to the HOMELESS DUDE. Smiles at him.

HOMELESS DUDE Come on, just gimme that money . . .

GUY You crazy?! *No!* I'm teaching you to *fish*, my man—don't you know that analogy? It's that one with the . . . how's it go?—"give a man a fish and he . . . but if you teach him to fish, then . . ." Fuck! I don't remember exactly, but basically you learn how to fish and you can take care of yourself. Get it? (*To his girlfriend.*) Right?

The other two people are silent. Staring over at him.

GUY Screw it, it's my money, take the bet or forget about it. You want the cash—pick which hand it's in.

HOMELESS DUDE . . . I can do that . . .

GUY *But*.

HOMELESS DUDE "But" what? Why you gotta say "but" to me now? Huh? Why?

GAL Clark, I don't like this, ok? You're . . .

GUY And you don't have to "like it," *okay*?! Just stand there and look gorgeous for another few seconds and I'll be done.

She's getting frustrated and the cold is getting to her—she starts rubbing her hands up and down along her arms and stamping her feet.

GAL Maybe I'll just go . . .

GUY *Where*? You didn't even bring a *purse*—don't think I didn't
notice—so I'm the money guy tonight and now this dude wants
some—for free—just because he's so, so *great* or something
and so fine, I'm now giving him the chance to have some . . .
do you mind? Can you hold on for a few more minutes without
complaining just once in our *entire* dating life?

GAL Clark! Don't talk to me like that.

GUY OK! Here. God. (*Takes off jacket, puts it over her shoulders.*)
Better? *Now* can I get on with this, please?

GAL . . . yes. Go on.

GUY Thank-you. (*To* HOMELESS DUDE.) Women, huh?

The GUY *looks around for a moment, up and down the street they're
on. It's nice and empty, for a big city.*

GAL . . . Clark . . .

The GUY *waves a dismissive hand at her, in effect telling her to
"be quiet." He turns back to the* HOMELESS DUDE.

GUY Okay, like I said "pick the hand it's in and the money's yours."
However: you get it wrong, I get to punch you. *One* time. Anywhere I want.

HOMELESS DUDE *What the fuck*?! Hold up, now . . . just hold on . . .

GAL Stop it. Clark, just stop it!

GUY I'm not doing anything! I'm suggesting a bet—if anything
happens . . . it's because this guy goes for it. (*To* HOMELESS DUDE.)
If you've got the guts, go ahead.

The HOMELESS DUDE *looks carefully at both of them.* GUY *flashes the money at him, smiles.*

He puts his hands behind his back and mixes it up again. His fists come back out front.

GUY . . . what's it gonna be, *Denzel*? You up for this or not?

GAL Stop calling him that!

GUY How do I know that's not his name? They like names like that. (*To* HOMELESS DUDE.) So what is it, then? T'Shawn? Julius? *Magic*, maybe?

GAL Clark, now you're just being . . .

HOMELESS DUDE It's Clark. Just like you, man.

GUY Bullshit! It is *not*!

HOMELESS DUDE 'S true. I was born "Clark" Jackson . . .

GUY Ok, well, at least you've got a classic last name. I was gonna say . . .

GAL Please can we just go? Just give the guy some money and let's head home . . .

GUY Nope. Ol' Clark and me are gonna finish this first. (*To* HOMELESS DUDE.) You ready to try or are you a coward, too . . . on top of being a fucking *beggar*? Hmmm?

HOMELESS DUDE Fine. I'll try it.

GUY Yeah? Even with the, you know . . . (*Making a punching move with both hands.*) Ya sure?

HOMELESS DUDE Yeah, man, I'm sure.

GUY Go for it, then, buddy. You take a really good guess now . . .

The GUY *holds out both hands. Turning them over slowly.*

The HOMELESS DUDE *studies both fists. About to choose one, then the other. Finally goes with the right. Taps on it with a dirty finger.*

GUY Hey, hey! What'd I say about touching me!

The GUY *pulls away but reluctantly opens his hand to show the crumpled legal tender.*

The HOMELESS DUDE *scoops it up, happy with himself. The* GAL *rolls her eyes.*

GAL All that for a *dollar*! Don't be such a bully, Clark. Now let's go . . .

The HOMELESS DUDE *shuffles away, counting his good fortune this evening. Or morning. The* GUY *calls him back:*

GUY Wait, man, hold up! (*Smiles.*) We just got started—double or nothing?

The HOMELESS DUDE *studies him. Looks at the single in his hand.*

GAL No, no, no! I'm not standing here for . . .
GUY Stop! Just—I'm almost done. (*To* HOMELESS DUDE.) Again? Here, let's make it at least interesting.

Without hesitation, the GUY *pulls a twenty off his roll and folds it up into a tiny square.*

GUY *There.* Now you got something to play for! *If* you've got the stomach for it . . .

GAL Clark, I'm seriously walking away now . . .

GUY So go, then! I'm doing something here.

The GAL *takes a couple steps but there's not really any place for her to go. She stops and looks back.*

GAL I can't believe you're acting . . . *so* . . .

GUY Believe it. I'm sick of being stopped all the time, every *five* minutes, them asking for my money, a cigarette, whatever. Time for it to stop. (*To* HOMELESS DUDE.) So: up to you, *Cassius Clay*— I made the bet. Are you man enough to take it?

HOMELESS DUDE . . . Hell yes . . .

GUY Cool. But remember it's double or nothing this time, so that's *two* punches. Just so we're clear.

The GUY *smiles at the* HOMELESS DUDE. *Puts his hands out. The* HOMELESS DUDE *studies his hands, then picks one.*

The GUY'*s palm is empty. Before the* HOMELESS DUDE *can even react a sharp right jab to his cheek knocks him on his butt.*

HOMELESS DUDE Aaawwwgghhh!

GUY Tough luck, buddy. Nice try, though. And now here's number two . . .

HOMELESS DUDE Please, man, please no! *Please*!!

GUY Come on, don't be such a . . .

GAL Clark, stop! STOP IT NOW!! STOP!!!

The GAL *is so persuasive in her yelling that the* GUY *stops an inch from hitting the* HOMELESS DUDE. *She grabs his arm and he turns to her.*

GUY *What*?!

GAL If you touch him once more—I mean, even *breathe* on him or whatever—I'm so outta here that you'll never see me again. And I mean "ever." For *all* time. (*Beat.*) Look at you, what you're doing . . . my God, you are acting like an, an animal! A *jungle* animal who's gone nuts in the head. I'm serious! I've had my doubts about you, I mean in the last few weeks, you have gone outta your way to be rude and mean and, and a real *scumbag* to waiters and cops and even people we know . . . I do not get what has gotten into you, seriously, I mean, like, *ever* since we slept together you have not been the same guy I met at that wine bar . . . I don't *get* it but I'm definitely *aware* of it. (*Beat.*) Now, I need ya to suck it up and be the guy I fell for . . . just turn away from this or I'm telling you now . . . I'm outta here if I have to *walk* all the way back to Fulton Street on my own! I will and that'll be the absolute end of us. You got that? I am deadly serious here—we're done if you don't follow me outta here right *now*. Up to you. (*Beat.*) Be a real man, someone I'm proud of, or keep being this . . . asshole that you're working so hard at tonight! And *Cancun* is off . . . just so you know. No way would I ever go to a foreign country with you now until you take a few anger management classes and maybe even some racial sensitivity thingie—a *seminar* or whatever. I'm just really not feeling safe around you and, so, just . . . prove me wrong or I walk away. Right now. (*Beat.*) I mean it, Clark. *Now*.

GUY Come on. *Rebecca*. (*Beat.*) That's bullshit.

GAL (*Bursts out crying.*) I guess that's my answer . . . okay! You are being such a bastard to me . . . *fine*!! I've wanted to break up with you for a while now and this is the perfect excuse!! I don't even need one for a, a *freak* like you but fine . . . you want one then you got one! That is it and I am done with you!! You hear me? I'm . . . I'm . . . *done*! Goodbye!!

And with that she's gone. Tottering off on her heels into the night. The GUY *looks at the* HOMELESS DUDE.

GUY Now look what you've done! Damnit!! I'll deal with you in a
second . . .

The GUY *curses to himself and starts to go after her as she disappears
out of sight.*

The HOMELESS DUDE *rubs his cheek. Checks to make sure his dollar
bill is safe.*

GUY Becca! Come on, stop for a—Becca! I was just trying to
help the guy! STOP!! Come back, Rebecca! STOP!! THIS IS *SO*
STUPID!!

The GUY *kicks over the* HOMELESS DUDE'*s cart, just for the effect. The
noise is deafening in the quiet neighborhood.*

The GUY *makes his way back to the* HOMELESS DUDE, *who turns and
looks at him. A long pause between them.*

GUY . . . ok for you, buddy—now you're gonna get it.

HOMELESS DUDE Get what?

GUY Duh. (*Breaks into a big grin.*) Your money! And thanks!! You
done good, my man.

HOMELESS DUDE Pleasure, bro . . .

GUY No kidding! (*Beat.*) You know how *hard* she was making it to
break up with her? Damn, I was having to be *such* a dickwad! It
was exhausting!

HOMELESS DUDE Sorry, man . . . I know how girls can be . . .

GUY (*Nodding at this.*) Not enough to just have laughs and get a pizza and, and, like, make out on a semi-regular basis! Who's not happy with that? *I* am! *All* guys are!

HOMELESS DUDE Sounds good to me.

GUY Exactly! Guys *want* that! But not girls . . . They want all that other . . . I mean, some gals just don't ever get the message, no matter how many *flares* you fire up there into that night sky. Two, three dozen, it doesn't matter. They just do-not-get-it. Especially the beautiful ones! I mean . . . yes, ok, you're great-looking! You *still* don't shut up at night . . . you *still* like bad movies and you *still* leave your shit all over the house! (*Beat.*) I dunno, man, I *really* do not know. Girls are weird . . .

The GUY *shakes his head, then counts out some money into the* HOMELESS DUDE*'s hand.* HOMELESS DUDE *studies it.*

HOMELESS DUDE Absolutely. (*Counting.*) I thought we said "sixty." When you came outside earlier . . .

GUY Did we?

HOMELESS DUDE We certainly did.

GUY Really? No, I thought it was . . .

HOMELESS DUDE Yes, you said "sixty" plus anything that I won off you. During the bet.

GUY Huh.

HOMELESS DUDE You said it, bro, not me.

GUY Okay, then, *bro.* Sixty it is. (*About to give him some more money.*) Hey, you wanna play for it? Double or nothing?

The two men look at each other and slowly smile—there is a moment of pure male understanding between them.

HOMELESS DUDE Nah. I'm good . . .

GUY Ok. Your loss. (*Beat.*) You outta here now or what?

HOMELESS DUDE Yep. Probably gonna buy me a room tonight and watch the game. Knicks are in town and so—anyways, it's getting cold out.

GUY Yeah, no kidding! And I lost a jacket in all this, too—*Calvin Klein*! (*Beat.*) . . . oh well. Worth it, I 'sppose.

The GUY *yawns, checks his watch.* HOMELESS DUDE *starts to shiver a little.*

HOMELESS DUDE Be seeing ya . . . gotta go. Freezing my butt off.

GUY Yeah, cool. Sounds good. (*Holds out his hand.*) And thanks, dude. Couldn't've done it without you! Seriously, I *tried*!

The both snicker at this and shake hands. Another twenty gets popped into the HOMELESS DUDE*'s hand.*

GUY Hey. Consider it a *tip* . . .

HOMELESS DUDE Sure ya wanna "touch"' me?

GUY Ha! Yeah, that was pretty good, right? So I'll see you around. Enjoy tomorrow or . . . whatever. Your *life*, I guess.

HOMELESS DUDE Yep. (*Beat.*) Hey, you wanna go get a meal or something? I know it's late, but . . .

GUY Ummmm . . . no, that's ok. I mean, thanks for your help and all that but, you know . . . you're still, like . . . a *street* person.

HOMELESS DUDE That's alright. I'm fine with that. I can respect that . . .

GUY 'Kay, good. Thanks. (*Beat.*) So . . . yeah . . . take care, or . . . you know . . . enjoy eating *garbage* or whatever it is you guys do.

HOMELESS DUDE You too. Heading home?

GUY Naw, gonna go back inside—couple cute girls in there tonight, gonna check 'em out.

HOMELESS DUDE Ha! You white boys never learn!

GUY That is true! We never do—but we keep on trying, so that's something.

The GUY *yawns and checks his watch. He fixes his hair in a window reflection, then heads back inside the bar.*

HOMELESS DUDE Amen to that, brother. *Amen to that . . .*

The HOMELESS DUDE *smirks and then turns back to his money. Begins to count it. Whistling.*

Silence. Darkness.

A GUY WALKS
INTO A BAR

A Guy Walks Into a Bar had its American premiere at the Lucille Lortel Theatre (MCC) in New York City in June 2012 (as part of a benefit collectively titled *The Heart of the Matter*). It was directed by Carolyn Cantor.

TED	Eddie Kaye Thomas
CLEO	Emmanuelle Chriqui

Silence. Darkness.

We're in a club of some sort. Loud music. People dancing and drinking and occasionally trying to connect.

A guy (TED) *standing there with a drink. Doesn't appear to be enjoying himself but he's putting up with it.*

After a moment, a gal (CLEO) *comes over. Stands near him.*

When they start speaking they do so loudly, over driving music (the sound is there to set the mood but disappears once they begin. The shouting is just for theatrical effect.)

TED . . . don't do it!

CLEO . . .

TED Seriously. Don't. *I'm* not worth it . . .

CLEO What's that?

TED Nothing! I was being silly! (*Smiles.*) I saw you stop there and so I just . . . you know . . .

CLEO I didn't hear what you said, though.

TED . . . I was gonna tell you to *not* fall in love with me . . . to be careful.

CLEO *Really?*

TED Yep. Just giving you fair warning.

CLEO I see. (*Beat.*) Well . . . thanks.

TED My pleasure! 'Least I could do.

CLEO I mean, how was I to know, by stopping right *here*, that I might . . . actually . . .

TED Exactly!

CLEO Very kind of you, sir!

TED I'm just that sort of guy! (*Smiles.*) I've got this sixth sense about things and it was just kind of *rolling* off of you . . . in *waves* . . . how much you were wanting me.

CLEO . . . God, and I thought I had you fooled . . .

TED Hey, it happens! Just the other day I was saying that to some- body . . . or *someone*—is one of those more right than the other? In proper grammar?—I'm never sure . . .

CLEO I dunno. (*Beat.*) Does it really, though? Happen to you a lot? Yeah, prob'ly *all* the time . . . nice-looking guy like you.

TED Ha! (*Beat.*) Truthfully? No, almost never.

CLEO "Almost?"

TED Well, I met my girlfriend that way, but—sorry, no, wait, my fiancée, I'm supposed to call her my "fiancée"—other than her, though, no. No other times in my life . . . not even once. (*Beat.*) *None* times.

CLEO Ha! Except today.

TED Right! But . . . no, I was *kidding* with you just now—I was only playing around.

CLEO Oh. You were?

TED I think so!! I'm a little drunk, so I'm not completely sure of anything that I'm saying at any one time but yeah . . . yes, I believe I am. I did *not* mean to make you mad. Or upset. Or . . . any of the above . . .

CLEO I'm not. At all.

TED Cool! Thanks! (*Beat.*) You're very nice!

They smile and listen to the music. TED *bounces around a bit. It's not quite dancing, but it's very close.*

TED This is going *really* well! I'm *so* sorry that I'm not trying to pick you up!!

CLEO Oh. So . . . you really *aren't* trying?

TED Nope, uh-uh. Not at all. (*Beat.*) I'm here with business clients—see those Asian guys over there, in the suits?—So I've gotta keep a clear head, but really, I am not after you. In any way. I promise. *Or* anybody else . . . (*Shouts.*) "Hey, people! All of you can stop coming on to me right now! I am *engaged* here, so knock it off!"

TED *makes a hand gesture, "pushing" the crowd back a bit.*

CLEO Thanks for that! (*Looking around.*) Everybody seems *really* relieved . . .

TED Well, I was getting a little fed up with all their crap! (*Turns to her.*) Especially you . . . you need to keep your hands off me! I already told you. I'm not interested . . .

CLEO Sorry! (*Hands held high.*) My bad . . .

TED *pats her comfortingly on the shoulder. Clinks glasses with her and smiles. He is more than a little drunk now.*

CLEO . . . and thus your warning earlier. Right?

TED Exactly! Several warnings, actually, and all for your own good! To save you any sort of, like . . . *heartbreak* . . . down the road. Or later tonight, even . . . (*Beat.*) After.

CLEO Ahhhh. "After." (*Smiles.*) My favorite.

TED Yeah, you know . . . that's when people get a little bit weepy or whatever. "After."

CLEO You mean "after" all the . . . (*Makes a few hand gestures.*) . . . good stuff.

TED Yeah. Later tonight or even, maybe . . . the next morning if they decide to, you know.

CLEO That's when "people" get upset usually? Is that what you've discovered . . . ?

TED It's been known to happen. (*Beat.*) I mean, to *others*. People who do those things . . . you know, behind the back of loved ones. Whom they've already made commitments to.

CLEO I see. But not *you*?

TED Virtually unheard of with me! And since I've been engaged— which I am, in case you didn't catch that before—not even one time. That's *zero* number of times.

CLEO Interesting.

TED Simple fact, really. That's all. I'm the faithful type. (*Beat.*) Yep.

CLEO Which is why you . . . pointed it out before?

TED Yes! Exactly! *Now* you're catching on!

CLEO It was more of a *humanitarian* gesture . . .

TED That *type* of thing! Not on like the scale of the U.N. or anything, but basically of a similar nature. It all springs from the desire to bring joy and do good things . . . same as them. Seriously. (*Beat.*) This is like one of those *peacekeeping* missions.

CLEO Ha! (*Beat.*) Ok, that's maybe a bit much! You were doing pretty good for a minute there, but now I think it's a little . . .

TED I know! Damn it, I had you going, right?!

CLEO *No!* (*Laugh.*) Not even for a second!

TED *Really*? Not just for a teeny . . . bit of . . . ?

CLEO God no! 'Course not. (*Beat.*) I mean, let's be honest here: this has been fun but if I said *"let's go upstairs right now"* you would follow me like a . . . lost little dog.

TED Nooooo! That is absolutely . . . *not* . . . true!

CLEO Oh, *really*?

TED Ahhhh, yes, really!

CLEO And why's that?

TED Firstly, there's a drug store on the next level, so that doesn't even make sense . . . unless this is a veiled signal for me to buy some *lube* . . . which is . . . just . . .

CLEO Ha! NO!! (*Beat.*) You *know* what I mean! To my "house," then! With me. To my place.

TED Well . . . that's obviously . . . different.

CLEO And . . . ?

TED *What*?

CLEO If I said that . . . *"let's get out of here and go to my place,"* you'd come with me, right? (*Beat.*) Wouldn't you?

TED I'd . . . no. I wouldn't! Plus, I'm here with people . . . my clients, which I already told you about. They're . . . *Japanese* . . .

CLEO Bullshit! And what does *that* have to do with anything? Them being Japanese?

TED . . . they come from a very *ancient* culture, so, no . . . they wouldn't understand.

CLEO I do not believe you.

TED Well, try me then. (*Beat.*) Go ahead!

CLEO Yeah, but . . . if I ask you now . . . you'll just reverse it and say "yes" and then I'll be . . . stuck with you.

TED Oh, hey, *thanks*!

CLEO You know what I mean!

TED Ummmmmmm, no, not really!

CLEO I was just making a point . . . before . . .

TED So wait, lemme get this—you don't *really* want to sleep with me or . . . do all the . . . ?

CLEO . . . what?

TED The other stuff! What you did with your hand gestures . . . before . . . (*He tries to copy her earlier gestures.*) All of the . . . you *know*! The "good stuff."

CLEO Ahhhh. *That* stuff.

TED Hey, that's what you called it! I'm not trying to be all . . . sexy guy . . . here. *You* said it first!

CLEO That's true. I did.

TED . . . you really did say it . . .

CLEO *steps a little closer to* TED. *Pressing in on him.*

CLEO But you would, though . . . right? If I asked you to. (*Beat.*) Come on, be honest!

TED What, go upstairs? *Directly* upstairs?

CLEO No, not to the drug store! (*Beat.*) If I asked you nicely to come home with me—

TED . . . and you made those hand gestures . . .

CLEO Yes! (*Smiles.*) If I did that . . . (*Makes a few more gestures.*) . . . then you would. *If* I asked you to. Correct?

TED *And* you can promise that my fiancée would never find out . . .

CLEO . . . not ever . . .

He thinks about this again. Checks his watch. She smiles.

TED *And* you will raise the child that will no doubt spring from this . . . unholy union on your own without any help from me, be it financial or . . . *fiscal* . . . or otherwise . . .

CLEO . . . those are essentially the same thing but alright . . . yes . . .

TED . . . then there's your answer! Right *there*.

CLEO What?

TED NO!! I can't!! (*Beat.*) See? You've already fallen in love with me! Why?! *Why* does it keep on happening to me?! WHY, GOD, WHY?!

CLEO No, wait . . . I'm being serious now! (*Beat.*) I know, I know, your fiancée and all that other . . . guys always say that kinda thing, the due diligence bit, but I'm gonna just cut to the chase now. (*Beat.*) You're cute, it's late, so why don't we do this? Plus all those first bits you said—the stuff that really does worry you about *babies* and her finding out—I'm down with that. This would just be you and me. One night only. No names. Just us, two strangers. (*Beat.*) This is not a *rebate*, there is no *coupon* attached here, so it's sort of a "now or never" thing. Ok? (*Beat.*) I know you're thinking "what-the-fuck or serial killer" . . . but I'm lonely, it's late, I drank a lot . . . so I'm asking.

The guy studies her for a second, unsure how to take what she's saying to him. Finally, he breaks out into a smile.

TED Get outta here! This is so shitty to do to somebody! (*Beat.*) *Who* are you? Do you know these guys . . . these Tokyo guys? I'm being serious now! *What*?! (*Beat.*) Wait . . . are you . . . come on now . . . hey. This is . . . but I'm . . . I *am* engaged! I told you that earlier . . . I'm already with someone. Else.

CLEO . . . yet you're still talking to *me*. (*Beat.*) Like I said, "now or never." And "never" is approaching like a . . . speeding train.

TED Then . . . you should . . . *God*!! (*Thumps himself on the head.*) Then you better go ahead and get on it, I guess . . . yeah, I guess so . . . you should just . . . jump on board and take off . . . *without* me. On that train, I mean.

She starts to speak but then disappears into the crowd. He watches her go, then stamps his feet. Shakes his head.

TED Shit! "Jump on board!" What are you, a complete . . . assbag?! I mean . . . come on! IDIOT!!

Suddenly she is there again. Staring right at him. He's unsure what to say but that's okay—she speaks first.

CLEO Don't say anything, just listen. That is your choice and I respect it. I do. All I want to say is that I'm . . . you know . . . I am surprised. That's all. You caught me off-guard, and I'm not saying this because I think I'm *so* amazing or anything—I mean, I am kind of great but that's beside the point—I'm just . . . I want you to know that I think you are, I dunno . . . I think that was cool of you and *rare*, you turning me down like that, and I just wanted to say that she's a very lucky girl and . . . yeah.

TED Thank you. That's really nice of you to say.

CLEO You're welcome.

TED Honestly. It is.

CLEO I just thought you should know . . . (*Beat.*) Okay, seriously. *Last* chance! I'll give you ten seconds and then I'm outta here!

She checks her watch. TED *starts to say something but she holds up a hand and makes him wait.*

CLEO *So?*

TED *hesitates but he doesn't bite.* CLEO *smiles at this.*

CLEO God, you're tough!! (*Beat.*) Alright then. I'm going now. I'll . . . just . . . yeah. (*Beat.*) . . . and . . . you're not even gonna ask me for my number or the . . . like, my *Facebook* . . . or nothing. Twitter. (*Beat.*) Are you?

TED I'm . . . I want to . . . I mean, sorta . . . but no. I'm not going to because that would be . . . you know. I *can't.* (*Smiles.*) I mean, if my girlfriend was out and . . . some guy was all up in her . . . you know? (*Beat.*) Not that I'm feeling like that about you . . . that you're *up* in my *face*, I really don't! But . . . you know what I mean. It wouldn't be right.

CLEO No, that's true. It wouldn't be. At all. *OK.* (*Beat.*) *And* if I told you this was a set-up . . . that I've known your fiancée for years, that we went to college together and just the other day we ran into each other downtown and over lunch she asked me to check up on you . . . to approach you when you're at work or at some business dinner . . . after you'd had a few drinks, and see if you would go to bed with me—I'd stop you, of course . . . after you'd taken your clothes off or put a *condom* on, of *course* I would—but just to be *sure* that she can trust you before she marries you, she had me do that . . . what would you do if *that* was the truth? Hmm? Would it piss you off? Would it make you fuck me if I let you, just to get back at her, the way I've always secretly wanted to get back at her for being *richer* and *nicer* and . . . you know . . . all those things that she is . . . more than me. (*Beat.*) What would you do with me if *that* is what's actually happening here . . . instead of us just *accidentally* bumping into each other by chance on this lonely Tuesday evening? Hmmmmm? What then?

TED . . . I would . . . you know . . . I'd have to give that some pretty . . . serious . . . thought.

CLEO . . . yeah, I know. I *know*, and to be fair, you haven't even seen me do this yet . . .

TED What?

CLEO *gives* TED *a big, passionate kiss. She finally stops.*

CLEO *That.*

TED Ahh. "That." (*Beat.*) No . . . I didn't yet have that important . . . bit of . . . info . . .

CLEO . . . have fun with your *clients*.

CLEO *exits.* TED *looks around the room, incredulous. He pulls out his phone and begins to call someone. Quickly.*

TED . . . come on, come on . . . ! (*Waits.*) Hey, hi there, honey! Hello!! I was just . . . yeah, I *know* it's loud . . . what? Umm, no, they're still *partying* away! But I wanted to call you because . . . I miss you . . . (*Beat.*) No, I wish I was there, too. No. Believe me, I *really* do. (*Beat.*) Hmmm? What? No, I just misunder—so what're you doing tonight? Huh? What's that? Oh, you've got another call? No, no, wait! That's . . . who is it? I said "who is it?" Who's calling? Is it anybody that I know? Sweetie?! No, wait, they can call back! *I* wanna talk to you right now, so . . . just wait! Sweetheart?! (*Beat.*) Hello? *Baby*? (*Beat.*) . . . hello?

He finishes his drink as he waits. Drumming his fingers on the table. His anxiety level growing by the second.

Silence. Darkness.

STRANGE FRUIT

Strange Fruit had its American premiere at New York Theater Workshop in New York City in June 2010 (as part of a series of short plays collectively titled *Standing on Ceremony*). It was directed by Brian Shnipper.

TOM   Matthew Broderick
JERRY   Jonathan Cake

Silence. Darkness.

A man (TOM) *standing in a bright light. Wearing a tux. He talks to us.*

Another man (JERRY) *in a tux stands next to him. Smiling.*

TOM . . . I love cock. I do. I'm really sort of just *into* it, you know? Cock. And that's what got all this started, I mean, how I ended up here in the first place. Because of that. The "cock" situation. (*Beat.*) And I had, like, *no* idea when I was younger, I really didn't! None. I wasn't secretly putting on my mom's dresses or make-up at night or, or, reading the *Hardy Boys* and getting a boner . . . nothing like that.

JERRY I loved the *Hardy Boys*, are you kidding me?! They were so cute, with all their . . . or maybe I'm thinking of the show. With Parker Stevenson. Yeah, that's it! That's the *Hardy Boys I* know. The TV ones. God, he was good-looking . . . *Parker* . . .

TOM Funny thing is, I was *totally* into girls when I was younger— seriously, I was!

JERRY I grew up in Oregon. Beautiful part of the country . . .

TOM So I did the whole "marriage and kids" thing when I was *nine-teen* . . . I did. Yeah! Why I don't know, because I was supposed to? Maybe. It was expected of me and so that's what I did. I did that . . . made it through six years. *Six*. (*Beat*.) No, "made it through" sounds so—and I don't wanna be like that, dump on her or be all—no, actually, it's pretty damn accurate!! I *just* made it through. *Barely*.

JERRY I met him when he was living in Chicago, divorced and just starting to dip his toe into the scene a little bit—totally not sure about what he wanted, how he saw his life going in the next however long . . . but he did like cock. That part was a given. *Oh* yeah!

TOM I already said that, didn't I? And it's true—second I tasted it, it was like a light went off in my head and all these, like, *fireworks* and stuff . . . big letters up in the sky saying "YES! WE'RE HOME!!" (*Beat*.) It was pretty awesome . . .

JERRY He couldn't get enough and I was, you know what it's like— hey, I've always been a very giving person! Who am I to stop a guy who wants to learn? And this dude just couldn't get enough . . .

TOM I just like the whole—the shape of the thing and how it's . . . the taste of it, I mean—not *taste*, really, it's only skin after all, how does that taste? But it's true, there's a certain—anyway, I'll shut up now! But you know what I'm saying . . . that shit is good! Cock.

JERRY Wow. I mean, yeah . . . he got really good at it. All of it. Sex.

TOM And somehow we sorta just stayed together and became, I dunno, a couple, I guess . . . I mean, pretty soon he was moved into my place and there we were. Him and me. This . . . *couple*. In a relationship.

JERRY I had always been looking for someone. I mean, a guy who I could be—you know what I'm saying! Someone special, who gets me.

TOM Anyway! Enough about us and the whole . . . trust me, it was working and if it does, *when* it does—in life, I'm saying—you shouldn't question happiness. Not ever.

JERRY He was just a funny guy, really. That's what I liked about him. (*Beat.*) And great with his kids—on the phone, anyway. He's not allowed to have them out to see him; they're in Orlando so he has to fly there if he wants to be around 'em at all, and that's . . . (*Beat.*) Did I mention that he's good in bed? Well . . .

TOM I do like sex!—I found that out pretty early on. Like, immediately.

JERRY And that's how it went and suddenly, you know how it is . . . like, five years go by! We're looking in the mirror one morning— we love to shave at the same time, share the water and, and the, you know, use the same little brush thingie with the soap— and, my god, I'm looking at myself and I say to him, I say "Jesus Christ, look at me. I'm twenty-*nine* years old." (*Beat.*) He leans over— doesn't say a word—just sort of lowers his head toward me, this little peck on my cheek. Then he whispers to me, "Wait'll next year. Thirty's a bitch . . . "

TOM He had a drop of foam on his nose, like a little puppy. Really fucking cute, if you wanna know the truth . . .

JERRY And we just stood there, bare-chested and with these towels on and started kissing. It was *so* good. Just—anyway, that's when he asked me. Said "Let's get married."

TOM Which was a big deal, right? I mean, like I said, I'd already done it before and it was, well, whatever . . . it was what it was. My kids are terrific. (*Beat.*) Anyway, we'd even talked about it before but living in Chicago it was always about *civil unions* and *domestic partnerships*, all this shit that wants to be the same, to give us a little hope that people are about to stop being so god- damn idiotic about something so basic, *so* simple if they'd just let it be but it's . . . anyway, he told me that he had this dream. About it. Like, a wish.

JERRY I just wanted it to be the same as anyone else, you know? Except two guys on top of the cake, in tuxes—really cute and both of us looking . . . it's stupid, I know, but I had *actual* dreams about it! Since I was a kid.

TOM We kinda just watched and waited, without saying too much about it and yet nothing at all was changing so we thought maybe we could move to another state or, or, you know—but years go by and finally I say it as we stand there in the bathroom shaving. I'm the one to say it but we're both thinking it. Let's make this thing real! Marriage.

JERRY Boom! Next day we've got tickets, we're off to California—there's a window out there for us, I mean, we're two active, informed, vibrant people, right? We see what's going on in the world and it turns out there's, like, this five month period in 2008 where that golden state near the ocean comes to its senses and says, "Yes, it's ok to be who you are" and we run out there like everyone else. Do this thing before anybody can say "no" to us again. And they do, they close that thing down like a book snapping shut, a few months later. Bam! But we do it. We get married.

TOM We looked amazing—I mean, yes, it was just the courthouse and all, but we did the whole deal he'd been wanting. Tuxes and, and just the entire—we were pretty much awesome. Standing there in the hall and . . . well, people were staring. That's all I'm gonna say. They were. *Staring.*

JERRY Just like I'd dreamed about. Seriously.

TOM And we were just giddy the rest of the day. This was in September and we snuck off to San Diego to be at that hotel that was in the movie with Marilyn Monroe and the guys dressing up like two women . . . you know the one! It's, ummmmm . . .

JERRY I'd never been to the Hotel Del Coronado. Just gorgeous, this
big ol' place propped up on the beach there . . . just very . . .

TOM I took my tux off but I could not get my husband—or *wife* or
whatever the hell I was gonna call him now—he wouldn't take his
off! Said he was gonna go downstairs and get some cigarettes . . .

JERRY My one vice.

TOM He'd been a smoker for years—works out *religiously* but
wouldn't think of giving up his nicotine! (*Smiles.*) He was standing
there, at the door to the room, smiling at me, this big grin on his
face. Asking me if I wanted anything. Some Twinkies or whatever.

JERRY Somebody loves "Hostess." It's true . . .

TOM I said "No thank you, I'm a married man now . . ." and we
laughed and I blew him a kiss. Out he went.

JERRY They didn't have any Marlboros there in the little gift shop
so I went out into the streets. Looking for a 7-11.

TOM And . . . apparently . . . he ran into three guys who were
coming up from a swim. Just some college kids from what the
news said . . . and the police report.

JERRY I was walking along in my tux, carrying a bag of *mangoes*
and one of those stupid roses that you buy—the single ones with
a bit of plastic around the petals—they keep 'em right up there by
the checkstand so I got one for my fella . . .

TOM And they must've said something because I know that . . . he
could never let shit go . . . you know? *Ever*. Some guy two feet
taller than him and ten years younger and he'd go after 'em like a
little *rooster* if it was about us or being gay or, like, any of the stuff
he believed in. Those kids in *Africa* or, or Amnesty International—
he'd be up in your face and telling you that you're full of shit!
(*Laughs.*) That was just him. You know?

JERRY I remember these surfer boys passing . . .

TOM He wasn't found until the next morning. Down by the rocks, where the water runs up onto the beach . . .

JERRY It's just funny . . . one day I'm standing in New York, the next thing you know I'm walking down a street with palm trees on it! I mean, *palm* trees!! With a rose in my hand and a paper bag full of strange fruit and, I dunno, this . . . love, I guess. Yeah, love in my heart for him and everybody else. Right? Even the three guys who are moving toward me now, three boys who are getting louder as they come . . .

TOM The story made the papers and was kind of a big deal, especially after all the . . . anyway. Yeah. (*Beat.*) One day, few months later, somebody sent me a picture of us, before all that, standing on the courthouse steps as we waited in line to go in—and I keep it out where I can see it now; I'll give it a glance when I head off to work or out for a run, that kinda thing—it's of the two of us, both in our suits and smiling and from a distance or, if you stand back from it just a bit . . . you know what?

JERRY I couldn't see their faces but they were laughing and the sun was just behind them as they came closer . . . laughing at *me*.

TOM We're like that couple you see on top of a cake. That little plastic couple, only it's two guys. *Us*. Vibrant and young and frozen for a moment. I mean . . . well, you get what I mean, right?

For a moment, the two men come together as one—hands held tight and smiling out toward the audience.

TOM Us standing there and smiling, as if all was right with our lives and not anything could possibly go wrong. You know?

JERRY They were laughing and it was getting louder but to me, on this day and how I was feeling . . . it sounded like birds singing . . .

TOM As if nothing in the whole wide world was able to scare us or hurt us or frighten us . . .

JERRY These beautiful little birds . . . singing just to me from up in Heaven above . . .

TOM No, not us. Not ever again . . .

Suddenly a light over JERRY *blinks off and out. He is now lost in the darkness.*

Their hands unlock. TOM *stands alone in the fading light.*

He tries to smile but this too fades away.

Silence. Darkness.

OVER THE RIVER AND THROUGH THE WOODS

Over the River and Through the Woods will have its American premiere in New York City at the Planet Connections Theater Festivity in June 2013.

A living room. Spartan furnishings. Not because of money but by choice. Scandinavian design.

TWO WOMEN *on the couch. Not talking but staring at each other. One older, one younger. A tea service nearby.*

The OLDER ONE *speaks first:*

THE OLDER . . . tell me again.

THE YOUNGER I can't.

THE OLDER You *can't* or you won't?

THE YOUNGER . . . I dunno . . . I just . . .

THE OLDER You don't want to say it or you really can't do it because it scares you and makes you sick . . . almost sick to your stomach. Like that kind of "can't?"

THE YOUNGER I'm . . . not sure. Both, I guess.

THE OLDER I see. (*Beat.*) Alright. I see.

THE YOUNGER I don't . . . that's not really something I wanna do right now. Go through all that. Not again.

THE OLDER Why?

THE YOUNGER . . .

THE OLDER No, I'm just asking you "why" because I mean, if it is true, if what you've said is true and we go through with this, you are gonna be asked about it two *hundred* times more . . . dozens and dozens of times and by different people. By *men*. Lots of men you don't even know and they will not all be friendly to you— *I* know you . . . I'm connected to you, *related* to you and care about you—but they won't. None of them will.

THE YOUNGER I know that . . . but . . . they're . . .

THE OLDER Many of them will be *wanting* to make you say it over and over and over again, all the things you told me and in even more detail . . . *greater* detail . . . and not because they believe you and want to help you—whereas *I* do . . . I *want* to help— but they will try to trip you up and say you're a liar and bring you down, that will be the requirement of their job, to do that, to make you fumble and cry and retract what you've said or taped or written down on paper. *That* is what's going to happen . . . if you continue on with this. (*Beat.*) I'm just telling you so that you fully know what you're getting in to. (*Beat.*) Okay?

THE YOUNGER Yes. I understand.

THE OLDER You do?

THE YOUNGER I do, yes.

THE OLDER I'm saying this for you. *Warning* you.

THE YOUNGER I know.

THE OLDER Not for me. Or him. (*Beat.*) For *you*.

THE YOUNGER I understand . . .

THE OLDER I hope so.

THE YOUNGER I do. I think I do.

THE OLDER Alright. I just . . . because he knows those people . . . those men . . . has *worked* with them and been *friends* with them and, and . . . for all these years. So many years. They are his friends and they'll want to protect him . . . to help *him*, not you. Do you see?

THE YOUNGER I think so.

THE OLDER You do? You completely understand that? That your life is about to never-be-the-same-again, no matter what you say after that? (*Beat.*) I mean, even if afterwards you were to say "wait a minute . . . maybe all or some or none of that really did happen . . . maybe most or some or all of that was just a dream," your life will already be altered. Along with the lives of the other people you'll have brought down with this—myself and you and everyone else—I'm not even including all the other family members who'll be asked to talk or comment or *testify*, no, I'm not counting any of them in this—but that's what will happen *if* we make the call. Or go down to the station. Or hire a lawyer. (*Beat.*) Just so you know . . .

THE YOUNGER . . . that's . . . I guess I didn't really think about all that happening . . .

THE OLDER No, probably not.

THE YOUNGER I mean . . . I don't wanna make you . . . or my parents . . . hate me . . . I don't. I just need the truth to be . . . I wanna tell the truth about this. About *him*.

THE OLDER I know you do.

THE YOUNGER You do?

THE OLDER Yes, I know you do. I can see that. That you want to tell the truth. The *real* and *honest* truth . . . to be truthful.

THE YOUNGER I do.

THE OLDER And the truth is *so* . . . it's complex, you know that, don't you? It's so so hard to know *truth* sometimes. The *complete* truth.

THE YOUNGER That's true.

THE OLDER But that's what you need to tell me right now . . . here, with me . . . while there's time. (*Beat.*) You need to do that. You have to.

THE YOUNGER I know. I mean . . . I *want* to.

THE OLDER No, not "want," no . . . that's not enough. You "have" to. You have to do it . . . for all of us.

THE YOUNGER . . . right . . .

THE OLDER Please, sweetheart. You *have* to.

THE YOUNGER I know . . . I will . . . I already have once, just a little while ago I did, but I'm also . . . I feel like . . . I need to tell it to others, too. Other people . . . (*Beat.*) But I'm . . . I really don't mean to *hurt* you with this. I really really don't.

THE OLDER I believe you.

THE YOUNGER You do?

THE OLDER Oh yes. I do. I believe you.

THE YOUNGER Thank you.

THE OLDER . . . but you will.

THE YOUNGER What?

THE OLDER You *will*.

THE YOUNGER I don't . . . I'm not sure what you mean. What will I do?

THE OLDER Hurt us. Hurt *me*. You will do that . . . if you go through with it. (*Beat.*) You *have* to see that. To know it.

THE YOUNGER . . . I . . . I guess so . . .

THE OLDER You do.

THE YOUNGER I suppose I do.

THE OLDER I know you do. Of *course* you do.

THE YOUNGER I mean . . .

THE OLDER No, you know it will. You *know* that . . . and not just hurt. No. You will *destroy* us . . . *ruin* us. *Finish* us off . . . *if* you do this. Continue with this . . .

THE YOUNGER . . .

THE OLDER For something that took place—if it *did* take place—*so* long ago. *Years* ago.

THE YOUNGER But it did happen. It did. I promise.

THE OLDER And I believe you . . . you *know* I do. I am not sitting here and saying that you're a *lying* or *ungrateful* child or anything like that . . . you can see that, can't you? And no matter how *much* we've handed you, how much we've done for you or given up for you: you know only the truth matters to me. Isn't that right? You *know* that.

THE YOUNGER Yes.

THE OLDER And you trust me, don't you?

THE YOUNGER I do. I really do.

THE OLDER You do?

THE YOUNGER Yes.

THE OLDER Please tell me if you don't . . .

THE YOUNGER No, I *do* . . . that's why I've . . . I came to you because of that . . . *because* I do . . .

THE OLDER Because if you don't—and I can even see why you might not, understand why you'd be afraid—but if you are or don't *like* me, *believe* in me, then we should . . .

THE YOUNGER Of *course* I do. I mean, I said it to you. Not my folks or any of my friends . . . you are the only person I've told.

THE OLDER Oh.

THE YOUNGER . . . so . . .

THE OLDER Just me?

THE YOUNGER Yes. You. I called you and . . . then . . .

THE OLDER Really? Is that true?

THE YOUNGER Absolutely. I came to you with it.

THE OLDER No one else?

THE YOUNGER No one.

THE OLDER Not even a boyfriend or, or, or just . . . someone from that job of yours?

THE YOUNGER   . . . I don't have a *boyfriend* . . .

THE OLDER   That's right, of course . . . I'm sorry . . .

THE YOUNGER   . . . it's alright . . .

THE OLDER   And no one else? Don't you see a social worker or someone? That woman . . . ?

THE YOUNGER   My therapist?

THE OLDER   Yes. Her. That's what I mean. *Therapist*.

THE YOUNGER   She's . . . yes, I do go there a few times a month . . .

THE OLDER   Surely you've told her about all this . . .

THE YOUNGER   . . . no, I haven't.

THE OLDER   *No*?

THE YOUNGER   Not yet. I haven't yet . . . *but* . . .

THE OLDER   Why not?

THE YOUNGER   I wanted . . . I thought I should talk to you first . . .

THE OLDER   That's right . . . we're family.

THE YOUNGER   Yes.

THE OLDER   We're connected.

THE YOUNGER   True.

THE OLDER   By blood. You and I have the *same* blood in us. *Flowing* through us . . .

THE YOUNGER   Yes . . . and, and . . . and I *love* you . . .

THE OLDER   I love you, too. You know that, right?

THE YOUNGER   Yes.

THE OLDER   And I would *never* hurt you . . . or let you be hurt . . .

THE YOUNGER   . . . no . . .

THE OLDER   So you know you can tell me . . .

THE YOUNGER   I can.

THE OLDER   . . . tell me everything . . .

THE YOUNGER   Yes.

THE OLDER   . . . about what happened.

THE YOUNGER I can. Yes. (*Beat.*) I have.

THE OLDER But . . .

THE YOUNGER What?

THE OLDER Nothing . . . ever happened *here*, did it? I mean . . . not really . . .

THE YOUNGER . . .

THE OLDER I'm not saying I don't believe you, but nothing did. Right? Not . . . at least not while I was watching you. Correct? (*Beat.*) Just tell me that much. That it wasn't—*if* something did happen—that it wasn't here or while I was watching.

THE YOUNGER No.

THE OLDER I don't know what that means. "No."

THE YOUNGER Not here . . . but . . . no, not in the house. I mean, not this house. It wasn't here, but it did happen. (*Beat.*) He would . . .

THE OLDER This was at the cabin, you said . . . isn't that what you told me? Earlier?

THE YOUNGER Uh-huh . . . when we were camping. At night.

THE OLDER What we used to call "outdoors." (*Beat.*) My father would say "out-of-doors" to me, that's the way he learned it. As a boy . . .

THE YOUNGER I know.

THE OLDER I've told you about him. Before.

THE YOUNGER Yes. I remember.

THE OLDER That's what he would say. "Out-of-doors."

THE YOUNGER I see.

THE OLDER And so . . . this happened . . . you *say* that it happened to you . . . outdoors. Out-of-doors.

THE YOUNGER It did. (*Beat.*) Yes . . . but inside the . . .

THE OLDER When you were sleeping, you told me.

THE YOUNGER Yes.

THE OLDER When you were asleep. You were asleep at the cabin and it happened . . .

THE YOUNGER . . . that's right . . . or . . . or . . . *maybe* . . .

THE OLDER *I* remember when you'd come home from a trip up to the lake—you always seemed very happy. You'd run to the back door with all the fish you'd caught together and show me, drag them in on a line all slippery . . . across the floor . . . and you'd smile up at me. (*Beat.*) You'd be *smiling*.

THE YOUNGER . . . I was?

THE OLDER Yes. Not sad, but smiling.

THE YOUNGER . . .

THE OLDER Always. Happy and holding his hand.

THE YOUNGER That's . . . I don't . . . remember that.

THE OLDER Maybe not, but *I* do . . . all of you home from the lake and you'd be laughing . . . happy and excited and alive.

THE YOUNGER I can't recall ever being . . . happy. (*Beat.*) I've been— I mean, I remember that, the coming home with fish and being . . . I did like the cabin and the . . . the lake was—but when I was sleeping, I can remember waking up and seeing him there . . . not in his bunk and the others were asleep, my dad and my brother and . . . they were all downstairs sleeping . . . but not him . . . he would sit by my bed, on the edge of it and slowly pull down the . . . he would tug on the zipper of my sleeping bag with a finger to his lips, hushing me while he opened the bag, bit by bit, each *tooth* of the zipper springing open and uncovering me . . . and then his hands would . . . I already told you about this . . . his hands would be so warm and . . . and . . . and . . . *wet* . . . they were damp and he would . . . start on my tummy and the rubbing . . . it would go like this . . . (*Doing it to herself with one hand.*) Down and down and down . . . until he got to where he

wanted to be. That's what he would do. (*Beat.*) I was not asleep
. . . his breath was— I'm . . . I did not *dream* it or imagine it or
create it in my mind. It took me *so* long to remember this . . .
to figure it out . . . to see into the past and put the pieces of the
puzzle together, but I know now what he did to me. I *do*. (*Beat.*)
Up there. In the woods.

THE OLDER I see. (*Beat.*) At nighttime. Sleep time.

THE YOUNGER Yes.

THE OLDER When you were sleeping.

THE YOUNGER Yes.

THE OLDER *Asleep.*

THE YOUNGER Yes. I mean . . . no. Not asleep. No.

THE OLDER Yes . . . you said . . . *yes* . . .

THE YOUNGER No, *in* bed . . . not sleeping . . .

THE OLDER You said he woke you . . .

THE YOUNGER Yes.

THE OLDER From *sleep.*

THE YOUNGER I was . . . no . . . drifting . . .

THE OLDER But . . . you said you were . . .

THE YOUNGER No. I was drifting off . . . not asleep yet but in that
place where . . . I was *adrift.*

THE OLDER I see.

THE YOUNGER I wasn't asleep . . . no. I wasn't.

THE OLDER Alright then. If you say so . . . if that's your *version* now
then I was wrong.

THE YOUNGER I don't mean to be . . . but no. I was not sleeping.

THE OLDER Fine.

THE YOUNGER I wasn't.

THE OLDER That's alright. It's fine. I'm sorry.

THE YOUNGER I really wasn't . . .

THE OLDER I understand. (*Beat.*) And then . . . he would stir you. Right? He came in and he was . . . his actions stirred you awake. *Or . . .* ?

THE YOUNGER . . . I think so. Or else I just woke up.

THE OLDER You mean . . . how? *How* did that happen?

THE YOUNGER On my own. Or . . . maybe . . . I was already . . .

THE OLDER That's—I don't want to do this to you, sweetheart, be the one to . . . but that's different than what you just said . . . or said the other time, too. On the phone.

THE YOUNGER . . . *no* . . .

THE OLDER Yes.

THE YOUNGER . . . but . . . no, I just said that . . . he . . .

THE OLDER It really is.

THE YOUNGER No . . . I said that he was *trying* to . . .

THE OLDER It is. I wish we had a record of it to play back on the phonograph because it is a new version of what you said when you called me. On that phone over there.

THE YOUNGER No, I told you that. About him coming up the stairs to . . . up to where I was . . .

THE OLDER *Before* you said you felt his hand on you first. That's what you said . . . (*Beat.*) Not about the stairs . . . not about coming in or about the zipper. No. He was just *there*.

THE YOUNGER No. I'm . . . *no* . . . that's . . .

THE OLDER You honestly did.

THE YOUNGER Did I?

THE OLDER Yes. (*Beat.*) A *policeman* would say . . .

THE YOUNGER But . . . I called you and . . . no, that's . . .

THE OLDER I promise you did. And you just did the same again. Just now.

THE YOUNGER No, I said . . . that's . . . I *just* said . . .

THE OLDER . . . his "hand." "On me." You said it the first time that way and now he's just . . . there. Over you. (*Beat.*) It's different.

THE YOUNGER That's . . . no . . . (*Beat.*) *Really*?

THE OLDER Yes. The *facts* are different now . . .

THE YOUNGER But I'm . . . I mean . . . it still happened.

THE OLDER Alright. (*Beat.*) I'm just saying that . . .

THE YOUNGER It did. It *absolutely* did.

THE OLDER *Did* it? (*Beat.*) That's all I want you to think about, one more time before I get my purse and go with you, down into town and we talk to whomever you want to talk to about it . . . I'll go with you and vouch for you and stand beside you . . . but please just think about it: about what happened, *if* it happened— happened like you've said it did—and what people are going to say about you now . . . about the kind of person that you are. (*Beat.*) Will you do that for me? *Sweetheart*? Go in the other room and just sit there . . . sit quietly for a moment by his picture—the one up on the piano—and ask yourself what the truth is, what it really really is . . . and then come back in here and we'll talk about it. Again. One more time. Will you do that for me? But you have to do it *now* . . . before he gets home from work . . . can you please do that for me this very instant? Hmm? *Can* you? (*Beat.*) I would certainly do it for you, if you asked me to . . .

THE YOUNGER . . .

THE OLDER I would . . . so will you do that for me?

THE YOUNGER . . . I guess . . .

THE OLDER You *will*?

THE YOUNGER If you think that I should . . .

THE OLDER I do. I honestly do.

THE YOUNGER Then I will.

THE OLDER Thank you.

THE YOUNGER I'll . . . sure. I can do that. That's . . . it's just *hard* for me to go there . . . to go into my mind to all that . . . *stuff* that happened . . . but . . .

Suddenly the YOUNGER ONE *starts to cry. The* OLDER ONE *is quick to comfort her—reaching a hand out to touch her.*

THE OLDER Please? For *me*? (*Beat.*) It's like looking into the future . . . your very own future . . . but backwards. That's all it is. You'll just be doing it backwards.

THE YOUNGER Yes. I will . . . for you. I'll do it for you if you really really feel like I should.

THE OLDER I do.

THE YOUNGER Then yes. (*Beat.*) I will.

THE OLDER *Please.* Just think about all this again. What's happened to you . . . and what you did or might've done to *make* it happen. Weigh it *all* in your mind and then come back in. Right back here. To me. (*Beat.*) Where you're safe . . .

THE YOUNGER Alright, I will. I'll try.

THE OLDER Thank you, sweetheart. Thank you . . .

THE YOUNGER . . . you're welcome.

The YOUNGER ONE *gets to her feet. Goes out of the room.*

The OLDER ONE *tries to pour some tea into the cup that's in front of her but her hands are shaking too much.*

She puts a hand over her mouth. Her eyes growing wide.

End.

BAD GIRL

Bad Girl had its American premiere at the Lucille Lortel Theatre (MCC) in New York City in June 2010 (as part of a benefit collectively titled *Filthy Talk for Troubled Times*). It was directed by Neil LaBute.

YOUNG WOMAN   Alice Eve

Silence. Darkness.

Moody, low-lit club. A throng of people standing around.

A YOUNG WOMAN *near a table. Nursing a drink. She speaks.*

YOUNG WOMAN   . . . thing is, I broke up with a guy not all that long
ago so I'm, you know . . . yeah. I'm not really ready for too much
of anything but it's just kinda, I dunno, weird maybe, even at my
age, to be without someone. To not at least have that man who
calls me up and wants to take me out, even if I can't make it.
Maybe that's all I need. Is that. Someone to want me, or . . . (*Beat.*)
What I *used* to do, and this is so childish, I realize that—but if I had
a relationship end . . . and I mean if, like, *he* ran out on me or that
type of thing, cheated with someone: I would go out a few nights
later to the bars and look around—it didn't matter where—could
even be at a restaurant or maybe a car dealer or wherever, and
I'd find—there is no way I should be telling you this!—I'd go after
the biggest loser in the place and then I'd fuck him. Yeah. Not as
a revenge or, or, you know, any thing like that—and I'm not saying
the ugliest one or a mean guy, an asshole or anyone of that nature
—but just the guy who you'd spot—and you can find this kind of

person at nearly any place you go, the laundromat or in, maybe, *Walgreen's*, places like that are good—and I'd go right over to him and offer myself up. (*Beat.*) I don't mean like it was obvious or anything, not like 'here I am, take me now' or shit like that but just be really really nice to him and laugh at his jokes maybe, let him ask me out to dinner or even to a film—you can't imagine some of the shit I've seen with these guys, like with the *subtitles* at the bottom and all that! Ohhhh Jesus, I thought I was gonna die a few times—but that's what I'd do. I would do that. Go out on the date and then back over to his place, if he had one, and then let him fuck me. Fuck me as many times as he could or, or wanted to . . . do anything he might ever dream up—trust me, a man like the kind I'm saying here is not all that super-inventive, they just feel so lucky to be even near you that they cum, like, in two seconds most of the time and spend the rest of the evening on the edge of the bed apologizing to you. Seriously. (*Beat.*) Never *twice*, though, ok? Don't be . . . that mistake is one I've made so don't do it. It's not even, I dunno, not that it's *so* bad or like you're starting up some sort of relationship or anything, but if you see that kind of guy again—any kind at all, really, but definitely the needier ones— then you're just getting yourself in deeper. You know? I mean, I saw this one again, type I mentioned, took me to the local *aquarium* or some deal and then out for ice creams—whatever— we fucked that night. Like I said, how I described. Fine. Some- thing in me, though, and I've tried to go back and track it down, see what it was that was so different about him but, see, I left him my number. Yep. And of course, I mean, yes, he calls me again— picked another moment where I was feeling low about something, might have been about work or, shit, I dunno, but I said alright, yeah, that I'd see him for a second time. I think his name was

Chip. Yes, it was, because when I heard it I was, like, "fuck, what?
Chip?" Anyways, we go to Six Flags (you know, with all those
rides and games and things) which is pretty fun, I have to admit,
and the whole time he's a complete gentleman . . . no sense of
a "date" where I have to hold his hand or be all smiley, no, we're just
laughing and . . . eating pizza and a ton of good stuff, *but*: back at
his apartment that night, he's totally different. I'm serious. Just
more, and this is slightly, that's all, just slightly, but still—wants me
to undress in front of him and a little rougher going inside me, just
a few things that a girl would notice, he's like that this time. *And*
he tricks me! He does, he totally turns a blow job around on me
where I've been really specific in that I don't swallow—I mean,
only for a guy who's, not even just special but like "the one," you
know? "Him." Marriage-guy. So I've told him that, this Chip, he
definitely knows the rules and he says "ok, no problem" and so
I trust him to follow the guidelines and whatever, to just do his
thing and then, you know . . . right? But Chip gets all, I mean, he
is totally shallow breathing me here, as if we've just started and he
could go on for however long and then he's, like, blam! He quivers
and shoots a quart of his . . . I don't even like *thinking* about it, so
imagine when it goes everywhere, mouth, my face, Stones T-shirt
I'm wearing . . . ppplllttt! O-kay, that's lovely! *And* as I look up at
him, getting ready to head off to the bathroom to clean up, he has
this look on his face. Not a smile, it's not exactly that, but in his
eyes, this . . . sort of a *gleam* or something. The way a regular guy
might look at me if he'd done that. Some good-looking guy who
gets away with that kinda shit in bed or even life because of his
face or what he does for a living or maybe his family . . . Chip is
sitting there, off in the shadows and watching me, with this faint
little grin and his pupils flaring up . . . excited by what he's just

done to me. We don't say a word about it to each other and I leave not that much later *but* he hardly even seems interested in me after that—with all these big yawns and this continuous stream of "I have to work in the morning" just to let me know I wasn't invited to stay over. My Stones shirt is ruined and I'm sure I definitely downed some of his nasty jizz and *that's* what I get from my second date with Chip? I'm not welcome to sleep over for a few hours? *Nice.* So I'm just saying, and your life is your own so do what you wanna, but hey: beware. Okay?

She nods and takes a sip of her drink. Looks around for a moment.

YOUNG WOMAN   However, if you wanna fuck someone so so grateful the first time around . . . and I'm saying, like, in tears and shit . . . *that* type of grateful, then you so have to screw a guy like the ones I was mentioning earlier. You really really do. But yeah, be careful —just the one time. Oh, and they will totally eat your pussy, and as many times as you ask them to, so that's something—not that they know what they're doing down there but most times it's still good enough to be at least ok. I mean, end of the day, it's just *licking*, right? Anybody can do it. (*Beat.*) But yeah. That's what I've done sometimes . . . when I'm feeling down or I find out the dude I'm with is actually married, I'll go do that. I mean, I don't end up *dating* 'em or anything, I'm not crazy! Right? It's just a little thing that I'll do, like a habit, or, or, or—I dunno, what else would you call it? A hobby, maybe. Yeah, like that. This thing you do every so often, makes ya feel good about yourself, nobody's the wiser. It's a *hobby*. (*Beat.*) I know it's not the best thing, it's probably pretty dangerous and crap like that, too, I know that, so I do try and curb that side of me these days, I really really do. But sometimes I can't help it . . . I'm a bad girl. And honestly, there is nothing like a super lame guy with his cock inside of you and *sobbing* as he fucks you to make you feel pretty alright about yourself. It's true.

She stops for a moment, thinks about it. Shrugs.

YOUNG WOMAN   . . . hey, I'm not pretending it's the smart choice or, or, like, the most *adult* thing to do in the world. I'm just saying that it works for *me*. Ok? (*Beat.*) Alright then. Jesus . . .

She turns and walks away. Disappears into the crowd.

Silence. Darkness.

THE PONY
OF LOVE

The Pony of Love had its American premiere at the Drama Book Shop in New York City in November 2010 (as part of a series of readings by this author and the actor Thomas Sadoski).

MAN   Neil LaBute

MAN   . . . I know, I know, "it's not you, it's me." Right? Isn't that
      what you were gonna say? Something like that? (*Beat.*) Oh, you
      weren't? *Really*? It felt like—yes, you were! Come on, at least
      gimme that, benefit of the doubt here, lemme have that one
      victory—you were gonna say some stupid thing like that so I'd
      feel better or something—do you really think that would do it?
      Hmmm? That I'd then be able to put all this behind me, our history
      together, with a pat little phrase like that one? I dunno, maybe
      I would, if you really meant it and then I felt the burden of . . .
      whatever it is that I've been carrying around lift off my shoulders,
      then maybe that'd be okay. Maybe you should try it—but see,
      you're not going to now, are you? Now that I've suggested it you
      wanna do the opposite . . . that's your trick, your stubborn streak
      coming through so now you won't say it and I'll continue to feel
      like someone just took a dump on my shoes. That's how bad I've
      been feeling lately, like I'm walking around town with shitty shoes
      and I can't even lean over to clean 'em off, that's how much grief
      I'm carrying around in this heart of mine . . . and then on top of
      that, as if that wasn't enough, on top of it you throw in "when I see
      you I'm gonna give you a massive hug." What the hell is that?
      Huh? Oh, that's great, that's really—a "hug?" Honestly, that's

what we're back to now, square one? Even less than that, really, I mean, a hug is like what you'd give your retarded cousin in a situation like this one. "Here, Ben, come get a hug before you go off with the nice man." How could you even say that to me, someone you've been with—"been with" as in done stuff with. You know, I mean, like "stuff" stuff. Sex stuff. And liked it! I mean, that's what you said—nobody made you say those things, that shit was pillow talk, mostly while I was trying to sleep, actually, so I know it was honest. You whispered all those sweet nothings to me, hours worth, at least collectively . . . hours and hours of that crap and now it's come get your hug? I don't wanna be some ungrateful person here, but that is kinda fucked. It really is. (*Beat.*) I'm just haunted by this whole—what'd I do? That's what keeps swirling around in my head, hour after hour—what in hell did I do wrong? My God, it was literally a week ago—no, my mistake . . . ten days, it was ten days ago but that's still very recent—that you and I were a thing, I won't call it "a couple" because it's one of the reasons that seem to've set you off in the first place, having to name what it is we had but if we don't, if we go around calling it nothing or, or acting like it's just us sometimes getting together or we happen to be in the same place at the same time—then it becomes "the love that dare not speak its name" and that's a whole different deal—that is not the image I want getting out about me to the general public. It isn't. Not that that isn't okay when you're into that, doing that with some dude and afraid to tell your co-workers or your parents, then I get that and I wouldn't wanna face life without benefits and you can't get married or all the shit that comes with being gay—in my world a guy can date whomever he wants to (not me . . . I'm not gonna let him date me but there's lot of other choices out there) and I am cool with that—

but here we are and I'm in love with you, seriously, desperately in love with you and all the times we've shared—were you even awake during our trip to the desert, I gotta question that because if you were your mind would be, like, officially blown right now, mine still is, as in freaked out by just the sheer *momentousness* of the moments that we shared. Together. I am still reeling from all that and now I see you on the street today and you're with friends and I stop you and you've got that look in your eye. The "shit on my shoes" look and gimme the "we need to talk" speech that makes any heart, from some CEO on Wall Street down to a, a, a regular guy like me feel horrible. Absolutely horrible and aware that the end is coming, that I've come to the end of the line and there's not even the good part happening, I'm not gonna be scooped up in the loving embrace of God and taken off because it's the rapture—no, this is just you telling me, between bites of the sandwich you're eating when you call me later—I could tell that you're having dinner while you're on the phone, don't deny it because it was obvious—you're telling me that we've got to slow down, that you need some time and space and, and . . . I don't remember now exactly what the third thing was but you needed that too, I remember that there was also this other deal that you needed—was it maybe "freedom," or something like that? "Free to be yourself or whomever you wanna be." When did I wanna take that away from you? I don't remember us having a run-in about that—I do about the cable, about doing a dumb thing like ordering Showtime without asking you, I remember that, but not us fighting over whether you should have a free day with your friends or not having to text me if you don't want to—I send you cute little messages and those smiley faces because I want to, because it's a sweet and romantic side of me that I try to

express—you don't have to reciprocate if you're not feeling it . . .
there are no requirements here, other than you don't absolutely
trash my heart and wander off into the wasteland never to be seen
again or whatever—that seems wrong to me. You know? Like you
haven't thought it through properly. (*Beat.*) Hey, I'm just sad. I get
that way when I've been fucked over, done in by a person whom
I've trusted and had feelings for—that's just me showing my soft
side and there's no shame in that. None that I can see, because
it makes me human. Human and lovable and a creature of emo-
tions, not just some animal who's been programmed by society
and a lousy dad to hold in their feelings, to suck it up and not care
about your soul as it's crushed under the uncaring heel of some
chick you once trusted with your dog and your life and, and, and
even the password to your *laptop*—no. That's not me. You can
do this, throw me away or aside or in any of those directions that
you want to, but I remain a vital and loving person beneath this
charred, discarded carcass that you've left along the roadside to
die—I guess I really just want you to know that. That I am bigger
than that, bigger than the guy whose life you just crushed—I'm
a man who will bounce back, who will not stand afraid to ride the
pony of love again (I think that's an actual thing, that isn't a phrase
I just made up, it's an Indian thing, like an old-time Native American totem which guides me and gives me strength)—I will again
ride on the pony of love and not only that, not only will I jump on
and ride it again but I'm gonna zip right past you when I do—yes,
I will, you'll be relaxing there with your pals, maybe at the beach
and you'll see me coming way in the distance, kinda like Clint
Eastwood in that one Western, coming out of the heat haze and
just as it seems as if I'm gonna go on past you, as if we've never
met or at least been properly introduced, right at that moment

I'm gonna turn my steed—I'll make him stop and turn and back right up to your beach chair or, or towel or however you're arranged there in the sand, I'll do that and then I'll have this majestic beast lift his tail and shit on you . . . not you but on your shoes—what do they call those . . . the beach-y kind? Espadrilles? —he will take a dump right on your Espadrille shoes with the hemp heels and then we'll ride off, my stallion and I, off and into the sunset— or at least down the beach for a bit, so far and fast that you can't even spot us anymore. That's what I'm gonna do when I see you again. That's how much you have hurt me. It'll be an eye for an eye—or a shoe for a shoe, or however you wanna look at it—but it will be biblical, what transpires between us. It will be outta the Old Testament, the justice I receive! *Now* do you get it? *Now* can you understand how much damage you've done?! (*Beat.*) Then good.

In the companion piece to Neil LaBute's 2009 Tony-nominated *reasons to be pretty*, Greg, Steph, Carly, and Kent pick up their lives three years later, but in different romantic pairings, as they each search desperately for that elusive object of desire: happiness. World premiere at New York City's MCC Theater, May 2013.

Praise for *reasons to be pretty*
"Mr. LaBute is writing some of the freshest and most illuminating American dialogue to be heard anywhere these days . . . *reasons* flows with the compelling naturalness of overheard conversation. . . ."   **—Ben Brantley, *The New York Times***

$14.95   978-1-4683-0721-4

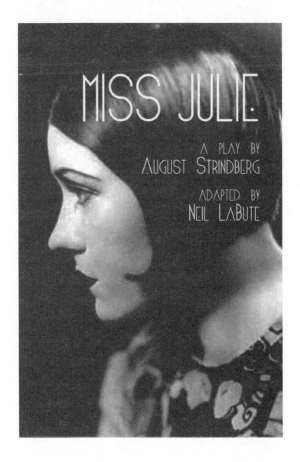